The Storm
is Passing Over

Roy Kerridge # The Storm is Passing Over

A Look at Black Churches in Britain

Photographs by Homer Sykes

47 colour illustrations

Thames and Hudson

© 1995 Thames and Hudson Ltd, London

British Library Cataloguing-in-Publication Data
A catalogue record for this book is available from the
British Library.

ISBN 0-500-27826-1

Printed and bound in Slovenia by Mladinska Knjiga

For John Davey

Contents

Contents

Preface

The 'Church of God' described in these pages is a composite church, not based on any one congregation or denomination. It follows therefore that its members are composite people and do not exist as individuals. The following names are fictitious: Pastor Spring, Sister Spring, Florence Spring, Arlene Spring, Anne Spring, Brother Clarendon, Sister Angie, Sister Hamilton, Sister Ruth, Brother Pullman, Sister Dorothy, Brother Hawkshaw, Brother Plummer, Brother Ray, Prophetess Porritt, Deacon Brown, Sister Jade. 'Jack Mandory, me name no one.'

In this book the term 'West Indian' is used in the English colloquial sense, and refers only to West Indians of African descent.

For their kind help and encouragement, I should like to thank the following individuals: Esther Abiona, John Michell, John and Vicky Harwood, Conira, Michael Wharton, Mr Chisholm, Anita Bright Bowers, Mr and Mrs Segal of the North West London Typewriting Bureau, and all at the Suman Marriage Bureau in Southall.

I should also like to thank Dominic Lawson for permission to reprint part of a 'New Life' column by Zenga Longmore from the *Spectator*.

The extract from 'When the Church of God Arises' by W. B. Blackburn is taken from *Banner Hymns*, by kind permission of White Wing Publishing House, Cleveland, Tennessee, 1957.

ROY KERRIDGE

Photographer's Acknowledgments

I am grateful for the co-operation and help that I have had from everyone while working on this book. Rarely have I met such a welcoming and joyous group of people, and it has been a pleasure to have spent time with them.

I should like to mention in particular: Senior Evangelist (Shepherd-in-Charge) J.O.Shebioba, Senior Evangelist Dr I.A.Haastrup, Senior Evangelist Ajih, Senior Evangelist Magbagbelola, all from the Celestial Church of Christ; Pastor Obi, Pastor Akigwe, Pastor Dr Amadi, Brother Henshaw and Deaconess Martha from the Brotherhood of the Cross and Star; Bishop Noel (1931–93) and Mother Twila from Mount Zion Spiritual Baptist Church; Bishop Poorman, Jeff and Guadalupe Poorman, and Pastor Reid from the Church of God of Prophecy; Pastor Lewinson from the New Testament Church of God; the Reverend Reynolds from the Calvary Church of God in Christ; Evangelist Hilda Steadman.

Kodak film was used for much of this project, processed by Paul and his team at Push One, Chelsea, to whom I am very grateful.

I should also like to thank Roy Kerridge. *The Storm is Passing Over* began as his idea, and it was his passion that kept the idea alight.

HOMER SYKES

Just as this book was nearing completion, we were distressed to learn of the death of Bishop Noel of Mount Zion Spiritual Baptist Church.

> I've anchored my soul in the Haven of Rest,
> I'll sail the wide seas no more;
> The tempest may sweep o'er the wild stormy deep;
> In Jesus I'm safe evermore.

GEORGE GIFFORD NOEL

BORN CARRIACOU, GRENADA, 1931. DIED HARLESDEN, LONDON, 1993

REST IN PEACE

CHAPTER ONE

How It All Began

Whether you believe it, whether you receive it,
The Lord shall come, and the earth shall quake,
And the mountains to their centre shake,
Whether you believe it or receive it.

(CHURCH OF GOD CHORUS)

About ten years ago my family moved to Kensal Green in north west London, a place I did not know very well. Lonely and brooding, I roamed the streets. Just at the bottom of our road was a funny little church, with red and green flags hanging outside. It had been converted from a shop.

'Mount Zion Spiritual Baptist Church', the sign outside read in spidery writing. Evidently the congregation were West Indians (a term I shall use throughout this book in place of the more fashionable phrase 'Afro-Caribbeans'). To my surprise, the haunting words of 'Go Down, Moses' wafted through the church grating and into the mellow autumn night. Rasta children whizzed by on skate-boards, but I stood enraptured as throaty harmonies poured forth, here a wailing solo, there a sudden unison of voices.

> God told Moses what to do,
> Let my people go!
> He parted the water and let them through,
> Won't you let my people go?

There I stood, listening, when a Jamaican housewife who lived in my new street saw me. Her name was Sister Muriel.

'Do you like that singing?' she asked. 'Does you believe in God?'

I answered 'yes' on both counts, so she swept me in and sat me on a chair. All the worshippers were surprised, the more so as Sister Muriel belonged to a different congregation. After a kind of flicker, as we introduced ourselves on request, the church rolled on. Bongo drums pattered, tambourines rattled and the Brothers and Sisters struck up another song.

> Jesus is a way-maker!
> Jesus is a way-maker!
> One day-ay
> He made a way-ay
> For me!

I looked around in wonderment, for the flickering candles in the long windowless room, and the many gaudy pictures, decorations and bunches of flowers, made me feel as if I were in an enchanted cave. On one wall, a mural depicted a grey wolf sitting beside a white lamb. In the middle of the room, a rough-hewn pole or tree trunk supported the ceiling. So many candles had been burnt out around the base of this tree that it seemed to have sprawling roots of white wax. Further up the trunk at eye level a prayer wheel with blazing candles had been fixed around the tree. Every now and then, Bishop Noel, the bearded Patriarch, an imposing man in scarlet robes, danced preachingly up to the wheel and pulled one of the maypole streamers dangling from it, to make it spin in a whirl of flame. I remembered having read of prayer wheels being used in the early Celtic church, when the old gods of Britain were still living memories.

Most of the other worshippers were middle-aged or elderly women, with very expressive faces. Not all were smiling and gentle – some looked stern, even frightening, with staring eyes between the crinkles, and high cheekbones. Some of the grim faces I saw around me recalled photographs I had seen of the weatherbeaten pipe-smoking Herrero women of the Kalahari Desert. Later I found that most members of Mount Zion came from Trinidad or Grenada, supplemented by Jamaicans, Small Islanders and a few Yorubas from Nigeria. All the women, except Sister Muriel, were resplendent in white aprons and turbans, with silk robes of blue, red, white or purple, trimmed with gold.

At the back of the hall, near a curtained-off Holy of Holies, a picture had been clumsily scrawled on the wall, showing Christ with a large head fringed all round with beard. He looked like a figure from an African mask. Some of the words of hymn-book songs, I noticed, had been altered. Instead of 'Heaven', 'Africa-land' was sometimes used. In spite of all this strangeness, the service seemed at heart to be an ordinary evangelical affair, with Bible readings and Redemption Hymns from the book. Only as we left did the church break out once more into an eerie chorus, amid swirls of incense.

> The storm is passing over, the storm is passing over!
> The storm is passing over, Hallelu!
> Hallelu, oh Hallelu!
> Don't you know the storm is passing over, Hallelu!

'Gather round the centre and pray, Israel!' I heard the Patriarch command in a hoarse roar, as he clanged a handbell. 'When you get near the pole, you don't joke!'

Wonderingly, I walked along the dark street with Sister Muriel, towards the little terraced house I now called home. Tales I had heard of sacred trees flitted in and out of my mind. Sister Muriel sensed my thoughts.

'That is not my regular church, you know,' she said. 'I am Church of God, and on Sunday morning you must call at my house and me take you. Mount Zion is a spiritual church – some might even call it Poco.'

'You mean, spiritualist?'

'No – spirit*ual*. A bit of Africa has stayed there since olden times in the West Indies. In my parish in Jamaica, they does call some o' these extreme churches Pocomania. Normal-like, I would only go in there if me prayer for illness or other trouble should fail in the Church of God.'

Years later, I discovered that by 'other trouble', Sister Muriel had meant witchcraft or 'obeah'. Some deeply religious turbaned women were adept at removing spells, but never put them on. Jamaicans called them Obeah Mothers.

No such ambivalence could be found in the Church of God on Sunday morning. Young people, born in England, made up half the congregation. Turbans, robes and Africa were noticeable by their absence. White shirts on the men, and white egret feathers on the hats of the middle-aged women, dazzled me by their brilliance, set against smart black suits and costumes. Again, women outnumbered men. None of them looked stern or frightening, though a few seemed faintly supercilious. Such a welcome I had never before received in a church!

'Welcome, welcome! We are deeply honoured to have you here! Sit down and feel at home! Stand up so we can see you!' cried the Pastor and Deacon in chorus, shaking my hand amid smiles all round.

Smiling foolishly myself, I took a seat and opened a hymn book straight on to 'Where Could I Go?' I could have been back with St Thomas's Youth Club Skiffle Group in Hove, the more so as many of the congregation came from the parish of St Thomas in Jamaica. Others were from Barbados. However, the style of the church, familiar to me from films and books, was black American. When the young people (nearly all girls) came to the front to sing, they used American accents. The headquarters of the church, staffed at the highest levels by white people, was in the American South. This church proved typical of most West-Indian-run churches in England.

I do not give the church's full name, for there is a whole family of Church of God denominations, all very much the same: Church of God in Christ, New Testament Church of God, Calvary Church of God in Christ,

Church of God Triumphant, Church of God of Prophecy, Humble Heart Church of God . . . I could go on.

Here were no handbells, incense or decoration. All was prim and Protestant, except the excitement of the music. The hymn book came from the Deep South. Thin-voiced Jamaicans and their children excelled at Country and Western hymns, while deep, earthy, soulful Barbadian tones added a vocal backbeat, breaking to the front with little wails and variations. Messages from the Bible were delivered with furious energy, the speakers jumping from the rostrum and marching round the rows of seats in their fervour.

A collection was taken while everyone sang a repetitive ditty known as a 'chorus'. Young women sat and jingled tambourines in unison, then with added layers of escalating rhythm. White English people, so fervently welcomed to the Church of God, will have to take up tambourine lessons if they are not radically to alter the services. Caribbean rhythms spiced up songs that may have originated in southern plantations or Wesleyan chapels.

> I've never been to Heaven but I've been told
> It's not made by hands!
> The streets up there are paved with gold,
> Not made by hands!

Chaperoned by Sister Muriel, pampered and petted by the congregation, deeply moved by all I saw and heard, it is little wonder that I became initiated into the Church of God. Now every year, I found, the Church of God holds a National Convention at Brighton. Glad to be back in the town of my fragmented school days, I walked down to the beach during the lunch break and saw a strange sight.

There, on the pebbles (for Brighton has no sand) a cloth had been laid, but not for a picnic. Large candles burned around the cloth, and in the middle of them, black men in white robes chanted and threw holy water around from lemonade bottles.

'Ask them what they're doing,' said young Sister Ashley, staring in surprise.

'We are an Apostolic Church,' said one of the men, in a Nigerian accent. He gave me his card. 'We have to praise God by the sea, for He made the sea before the land. When we are on land, our church is in London.'

'Oh, an African spiritual church,' said Sister Ashley when I returned and told her.

She seemed to dismiss the subject from her mind, but I could not. Although I knew the Church of God would not approve, I went to the address on the card and found a Yoruba church very like Mount Zion, if less exotic. Nearly everyone wore white robes. Men somewhat outnumbered women. Songs were in Yoruba, but most of the sermons (or 'messages') were in English. Fellow-worshippers seemed to take my presence for granted.

When the Pastor eventually returned to Nigeria, this little backstreet church closed down.

One of the members joined a similar denomination, the Celestial Church of Christ, or 'Cele'. I began to attend their services, held in a former Anglican church in an Islington square. One day, while praying with the Yoruba of Islington, I heard a startled child's voice call my name. It was little Sister Jade from the Church of God! Amazed to see one another, a West Indian and an Englishman among Nigerians, we compared notes. Jade's mother, an important Prophetess in Celestial, came from the Caribbean, but had married an African. In her school holidays, Sister Jade went to stay with her Church of God godmother. We were the only people we had ever heard of who went to both churches.

Christmas came, and at a big Church of God concert I swayed in my seat as the Mass Youth Choir sang, here a solo, there a tumbling wall of sound.

I must journey on,

The night is coming o-on,

And I am far from home,

But the storm is passing over, Hallelu!

Is the storm passing over for West Indian Christians in England? Often I had heard tales of the early days of Jamaicans in London, of rebuffs in the Church of England and of prayer meetings held in bed-sitting rooms, then in front rooms, hired halls and at last in newly-bought ex-Methodist churches. The fire that Wesley lit had gone out for the white British, so West Indians bought their churches to rekindle flames of Pentecost.

One big Methodist church had been wrecked by rooftop lead thieves. The organ had been torn out by brass-pipe robbers who had accidentally set the roof on fire, so the church was open to the sky. It was sold to the Church of God at the knockdown 1960s price of £4000. Members worked in their spare time to restore it, singing all the while, even as the rain fell.

Even now, the average Church of God meets in a hired hall, usually paying rent to a vicar. Rent is an ever-present worry, and concerts are held to raise the money. Flight from Anglican worship began in the early 1900s, in Jamaica itself. When the Church of God arrived in the Caribbean, brought from the American South by returning migrant labourers, the Country and Western hymns and gospel songs created a sensation. In vain, Jamaican vicars pleaded for deacons to return to the Church of England fold. Ecstatic experiences, holy dancing, Holy Ghost fire in the bones, became accepted forms of worship. Hitherto, when the Anglican and Methodist churches ruled supreme, such behaviour belonged to the humble spiritual and 'jump-up' churches. Songs from these churches spread into the mainstream. First the Bahamas and finally Jamaica succumbed to the Pentecostal fire.

On another level, the slight discomfiture of the 'nominal churches', as they were known in the Church of God, could be linked to the decline of

England and Empire. America grew in attraction as Britain faded. Even so, the Church of God in England is nothing if not patriotic. Gigantic Union Jacks are waved at Conventions, and the Royal Family are mentioned all the time.

'The Queen knows our way of worshipping is right!' a Church of God deacon told his flock. 'She would like to come here and worship with us, but she knows that if she did so, other subjects might despise her.'

In England, as many West Indians stayed in the Anglican and Methodist churches as left to join the fledgling Church of God. These stalwarts 'thawed out' the 'nominal churches' and have now claimed an equal part in them. No Church of God missionaries, and indeed no Church of God, existed when Christians from England came to the nineteenth-century Caribbean to convert the slaves and brave the planters' wrath.

Church of God life, as depicted in these pages, is *new*, both in Britain and the Caribbean. However, by the 1950s age of immigration, it was old enough in the Caribbean to have a hierarchy which could help, influence and organize the migrants in London.

Likewise, in West Africa, the Celestial Church of Christ and other similar 'spiritual churches' were founded in the early years of this century. Headquarters of such churches remain in the African towns of their foundation. Individuals – perhaps former Anglicans, Methodists and Catholics – began to have visions of uniting the Christian European and the pre-Christian African forms of worship. Visions appear easily in Africa, where every tree, rock and pool has a guardian spirit. In a spiritual church, a man can be a Christian without the strain of behaving exactly like an Englishman. Prophets, as imposing as those of ancient Israel, founded the African churches. They are a happy compromise of old and new.

Mount Zion and all the other Mounts – Mount Paran, Mount Carmel and so forth – have still earlier beginnings, the clandestine churches of slavery days. Similar churches, also called 'spiritual churches', exist all over the

American South and in South Africa. As far as I know, their resemblances are telepathic or coincidental. Prophets in such churches are guided by dreams, and services vary wildly. Sometimes the dreams are sent by African ancestors, sometimes they are inspired by the Bible and sometimes distilled from Anglican or Catholic memories. Churches of individual inspiration, they seem the oldest churches of all, their songs of interest to those who love old spirituals and who yearn to know how men worshipped God in golden ages long forgotten.

So here I present to you these three churches, Mount Zion, Celestial and, above all, the Church of God. What use is a voyage of discovery if I don't recount my adventures?

The Church of God

Here we see mainstream and highly typical West Indian worship in Britain. Similarities with the black-led churches of the USA and indeed with all 'born again' English-speaking congregations are obvious. Most members of 'Prophecy', 'New Testament' and the Calvary Church of God in Christ are of Jamaican or Barbadian origin. Many young people, born in Britain of West Indian parents, attend these churches with great enthusiasm.

On Sunday morning outside the Brighton Conference Centre, on the occasion of the Church of God of Prophecy National Convention (*opposite, above*), the Women's Missionary Band, or women's section of the church, line up for their annual parade along the seafront. They carry the church flag, which displays a sceptre to symbolize Christ's Authority, a star to represent the Star of Bethlehem and the Crown of Kingship. The colour purple also symbolizes Royalty, while blue is for Truth and red represents the Blood of Jesus.

Emotional preaching at the Convention calls down the Holy Spirit, who makes this Sister shout out in 'tongues' (*opposite, below*). She is 'in the spirit'. Quite used to this phenomenon, the brethren beside her calmly consult their programmes.

The children's Sunday School at Tubbs Road Church of God of Prophecy, Harlesden, London (*above*). Several Sunday Schools take place simultaneously, for all age groups, in different parts of the building. Adult Sunday School lessons are taught from books written and printed in Cleveland, Tennessee.

In the church hall at Tubbs Road (*opposite, above*), the Pastor and assistant baptize a young boy, with great solemnity. As in most 'born again' churches, candidates make their own decision to be baptized by full immersion in the name of the Father, Son and Holy Ghost.

Fiery preaching follows the baptismal service (*opposite, below*). Carried away by his message, the inspired preacher moves up and down the hall. The church drumkit in the background is ready for use when songbooks (*The Banner Hymn*) are opened.

As the red-robed choir sing (*opposite, above*), in the Calvary Church of God in Christ, a Brother can sit down no longer! Filled with the Holy Spirit, he dances joyously in the aisles.

Chorus time in the Calvary Church of God in Christ (*opposite, below*).

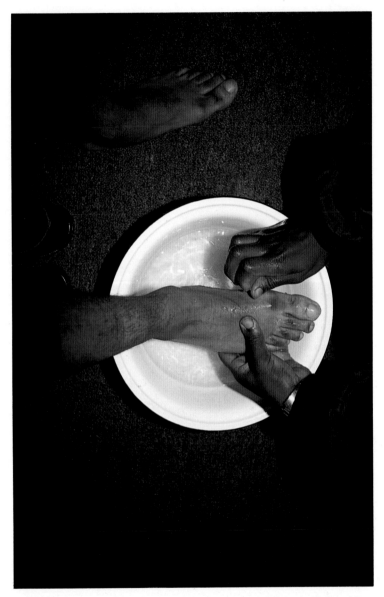

After the Lord's Supper, in the Church of God of Prophecy, feetwashing takes place (*above*), a practice sanctioned by the Gospels and also practised in some Roman Catholic churches. Members gently and lovingly wash and dry one another's feet, then kiss and embrace.

Prayer in the Church of God of Prophecy, (*above*): 'Oh Lord, we thank you for sparing life.'

Thousands gather at the funeral of Winston Patterson (*opposite, above*), at the New Testament Church of God, to pay their last respects to a well-loved Brother before his coffin is closed. A male choir sings 'Steal Away to Jesus', as members file by. Winston Patterson was a chaplain at Holloway Prison. Female prisoners, warders and the prison governor attend his funeral.

In St Pancras cemetery, flowers are placed upon Winston Patterson's grave (*opposite, below*), as mourners sing and pray.

Overleaf: **Evangelist Hilda H. Steadman** holds services in her East End flat, where the front room has been transformed into the Lily of the Valley Mission. Independent of any one denomination, the Evangelist is active in Christian circles all over Britain and in America, as well as in her native Jamaica.

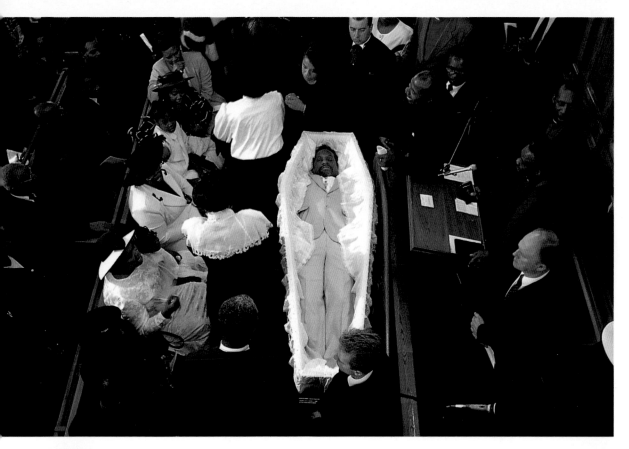

CHAPTER TWO

Praising the Lord: Three Typical Services

Praise Him! Praise Him!
Praise Him in the morning,
Praise Him in the noontide,
Praise Him, Praise Him,
Praise Him as the sun goes down!

The Church of God

Sunday School is just ending as I pop into the nearest Church of God for the morning service. I live in London most of the time, so my nearest church will probably be in that city. However, I travel about a great deal, so the church might well be in Cardiff, Sheffield, Bradford, Birmingham or Wolverhampton. Wherever Jamaicans, Barbadians and their children, the black British, live, the Church of God is there, the form of its services much the same in every place. There is only one difference – if the church is in the Midlands, where the black British talk Jamaico-Brummish, there will be as many young men as women in the church.

Why this should be, I cannot say, for the distractions of dances, parties and nightclubs exist in the Midlands as much as anywhere else, to lure young men away from the strictly puritanical Church. However, the zealous young men of Dudley, Willenhall or wherever, have made the Midland churches famous for their musicians and male and female choirs.

Just now, however, I don't happen to be in the Midlands, and the only musical instruments being played are tambourines and an electric organ, or keyboard. In the evenings, an elderly man might strum a banjo or a young man pluck an electric guitar. On special occasions, young Brother Clarendon staggers in with his drumkit. The song 'Praise Him' is a 'chorus', or short gospel hymn, repeated again and again with sizzling tambourine percussion. Tambourines are kept in a filing cabinet or 'press', and handed out to all who want them, mostly young people.

Each morning service is preceded by Sunday School, both for grown-ups and children. A ring of chairs has been set up in the corner for the Children's Sunday School. Twelve noisy children, aged from five to ten, are being encouraged to draw Bible pictures or answer Bible quizzes under the tutelage of the pastor's teenage daughter. A man of many daughters, Pastor Spring and his wife Sister Spring have raised a gospel-singing family. 'Heaven Harmonies', featuring the four Spring Sisters, is a frequent item at church concerts. Sometimes Pastor Spring plays an acoustic guitar. The girls also act in church plays.

Sunday School over, the chairs scrape and the children noisily take their places among the adults. Those who are too noisy find themselves hemmed in by stern elder brethren and constantly 'shushed'. Most of the little ones sit together and talk softly, comparing drawings and making paper aeroplanes out of their quiz sheets. Older men and women (or Brothers and Sisters) arrive constantly and take their accustomed seats. Strangers have their names taken by Sister Angie, the twenty-year-old Public Relations Director.

'Are you a "saved" Christian or not?' she enquires, and jots the answer down.

Pastor Spring now ascends four steps to the rostrum and announces, 'Greetings!'

'Greetings!' the whole church replies.

'Shall we say, "Praise the Lord"?' he continues.

When the rafters have ceased to ring, he asks the obedient church to pray for a successful morning worship. Everybody stands up and prays aloud in a hubbub of voices, in which the loudest predominate. Their inventiveness is remarkable. Nobody runs out of ideas, for there is plenty to pray about. Many bow their heads, but the Pastor and two or three respected elders glance skywards prayerfully, throats pouring forth supplications.

'Oh, Heavenly Father, we thank You, Lord, for sparing life that we can be here today to worship in Your Heavenly Presence . . .'

God is held in fearful awe, for He gave us life and lets us keep it on forbearance. At any time, He can take it back. Others fall silent as the person with the most imposing voice carries the prayer-poem to its final 'Aymen'.

Pastor Spring, a supple, well-dressed man, then calls on one of the congregation to 'take the Devotional Service today'. The Brother or Sister, who will have been tipped off half an hour earlier, rises to the occasion with two Bible texts and two hymns from the book already chosen. Devotionals ensure that every member of the church can get up and address the congregation over the course of a year. Those who wish can sing solos or preach for a minute or two, and so talents are recognized and developed. Prayers are now joined once more, and an offering is gathered to the tune of yet another chorus, 'Give It with a Willing Mind'. Some members take a brown 'tithe envelope', insert a tenth of their earnings and give it to the usher on his return journey, their names hastily scrawled on the outside. Others wave the usher away dismissively and give nothing. Most drop a large handful of silver into the plate.

Once collected, the offering is prayed over by the usher, as soon as the plate has been handed to the Pastor, Church Treasurer or Secretary. Young women are yearly appointed as church secretaries, reporters (for the church mag) and minute-takers. Everyone in the church has an office, even if only as 'booster' or Church Encourager. None of these posts, nor that of the Pastor himself, are paid. All have day jobs. Middle-aged men tend to work in Transport, women in hospitals and girls in offices. Teenage boys stay at college as long as possible.

Meanwhile the usher is still praying aloud over the offering, inspiration following inspiration.

'Accept our offering, Lord, come from your children's pockets, Lord; may it be used, Lord, only for what is right.'

'Yes, Lord! Oh, wonderful!' cries Sister Spring.

Another Country and Western hymn is sung from the book, of the type beloved of Elvis Presley in his gentler moments. The congregation and the usher sit down, and the Devotional speaker concludes, 'I shall now return you to the Pastor in care of the Holy Ghost.'

Greeting the church once more, the Pastor then makes his Announcements. Sister Angie slips over to him with the list of strangers and visitors. Each is welcomed by name, and has to stand shyly as the church gives them 'a good cheer'. This is not a 'Hooray' but a vigorous handclapping. Strong hands are needed in church, for in every spare moment a chorus is sung, with handclapping that never misses a beat. Some of the visitors are members of similar churches in far-flung British cities, or from Jamaica or Canada (where Jamaicans have settled). Most of the Pastor's Announcements concern invitations to and from other churches, the best singers and most able preachers in much demand. The Church of God has renounced 'the world' and forms its own closed world, a lively place.

Sister Spring, who has trained two generations of choir and solo-singers for the church, is an official Song Leader or 'starter outer' of hymns from the book. She leads out a strong first line in the correct key, and the church follows. Later, her voice may reappear in a repetitive background harmony, as with white spiritual singers of Bluegrass mountain melodies. Song over, the Message begins. Young Florence Spring, the fresh-faced keyboard player, leans forward across her instrument, hanging on her father's words. The three other Spring girls are equally attentive, their eyes glowing.

As the sermon proceeds, Sister Spring cries 'Ah, Truth! Truth!' at intervals. Far from falling asleep, as in the Church of England next door, the congregation seem riveted upright, the playful children a notable exception. Sister Angie, who is of Barbadian descent, looks more than ever like a Benin bronze, expressive features and swan-like neck. Older people, connoisseurs of many Messages, drink in the rise and fall of sound and the emotional gestures with deep appreciation. This is a middle-sized church, with perhaps thirty members of all ages present.

'God wake me up this morning!' the pastor cries. 'I look around, everything is so nice! Without God and the breath of life, nothing for us would be possible! Here we are, in 1993, still alive! Yes! I am glad! Let us all say, ''Still alive!'''

The church does so, in chorus, unconscious disciples all of G.K. Chesterton, the great Christian writer, who believed in seeing the world afresh each day as if it were newly made. No written notes are needed for Pastor Spring's address, only an encyclopaedic knowledge of the Bible, chapter and verse.

'Turn to your Bibles, everyone! When I say the verse, I want somebody to read!'

Members bring their own Bibles, the church geared to the King James standard. Bibles open everywhere, and somebody in the front row reads a selected verse. Pastor Spring, whose ebullient delivery precludes reading, repeats the line with dramatic emphasis, then adds his own thoughts upon it. Sometimes he wishes himself into the Bible, and addresses himself to a famous prophet.

'Moses! See the staff! Go on, man! Pick it up!'

Greatly inspired, the Pastor makes his way down the aisle, stamping a foot, repeating a text and giving a clap, one after the other, in jerky procession. Then he returns to the rostrum and rapidly travels the Bible from Exodus to 'John the Revelator'. His avowed theme is the contrast of God's goodness with Satan's scheming ways.

'The tree worships God! Don't you know the lion, fierce as he is, he worships God! He worships God! The ant — he is small but wise. He worships God! The ant is sensible!'

The passion of Pastor Spring's shouting delivery, so thrilling to the congregation, conveys a message worthy of Aesop or St Francis.

'If you take on pomps and prides, the devil get a foot in the door! Some gets jealous o' their neighbour, they forget God's love; they go to the obeah man [witchdoctor], get into all kind o' wickedness! Yes, man! All because of sin, all because o' that One-Suit Man! Ha! Yes, Satan was a One-Suit Man! He was thrown out of Heaven with only the one black suit him was wearing! I tell you something! I don't like that man at all!'

Only the small children seem impervious to this message. Instead of shouting 'Amen!', they solemnly put their fingers in their ears. Some members look sadly at an empty chair where young Brother so-and-so used to sit. When young men reach the age of thirteen, they become difficult to keep in church. Many become 'backsliders', permanent and much-prayed-over members in absence. Since a drink in a pub is looked on as Sin, defections increase as boys grow older. Young women are not affected in the same way, though some leave church for 'the world'. Usually they miss worship so much that they return and publicly repent, sometimes carrying a baby. Babies are very welcome and thoroughly fussed over in church. Some girls cannot face public repentance, and remain wistful outsiders looking in.

To understand the young man's point of view, I recommend a reading of Richard Wright's autobiography, *Black Boy*. Restless, hot-blooded, impatient of a Gospel of peace and purity, the young men of a Deep South church try to mask their aching boredom. The hymns and gospel songs of Wright's pre-war Southern boyhood are sung in the Church of God today – 'Amazing Grace' and 'Standing in the Need of Prayer'. At one time, I thought teenage Brother Clarendon was suffering from Richard Wright's Syndrome. He jerked and patted convulsively, as if bored out of his mind, a deadpan expression on his face. However, he later emerged as a mighty drummer before the Lord. Even now, during the Message, he absently biffs pieces off a plastic potted flower as he hits out drum licks in his head.

'Lively preaching' startles and sometimes repels English lovers of traditional liturgy. If a Church of God preacher tries out a formal style, one of the older Sisters might cry out, 'Loosen! Loosen!'

Concluding his Message, Pastor Spring addresses the 'unsaved' and by now uneasy visitors and urges them to give their lives to Jesus. This is an Altar Call. Long-standing members go up to the front of the church and kneel on stringy cushions as they renew their faith. Motherly Sister Spring prays over each one quietly, reminding us that, 'When the devil of hell come around, Jesus will rebuke the devil of hell.'

Usually the visitors defer their decision, remaining silently on their knees until released by the command, 'Rise by faith!'

After the Closing Prayer, Pastor Spring looks around and picks on somebody to 'pronounce the Benediction'. Whenever that somebody is me, I can never remember the way it goes. It begins, 'Now may the Saving Grace . . . .'

Morning worship is over, and everyone mills around, talking, laughing, discussing gospel concerts and showing wedding photographs. Members greet one another ecstatically, shaking hands over and over again, feathers on hats bobbing up and down.

'Sister Hamilton! So how you is?'

Mount Zion Spiritual Baptist Church

From the Church of God, we now move on to Mount Zion Spiritual Baptist Church, presided over by the flamboyant Bishop Noel. Despite the Caribbean trimmings, everything we saw at the Church of God has been recognizably British or American Evangelical. Nothing that happens there could surprise or disturb a Wesley, a Gipsy Smith or a Billy Graham. Spiritual churches, however, have an African form, unfamiliar to most Englishmen. Mount Zion, Mount Paran, Mount Carmel and the other

Mounts have the 'Steal Away' atmosphere of a transported African congregation who have slipped their New World chains by night and gathered to seek solace with Jesus.

In Mount Zion's heavily-curtained, candle-smoked half-light, with pictures on the walls and incense in the air, miracles hang unseen over the turbaned women and earnest men. Middle-aged members predominate, but babies in arms are never absent, taken upstairs by their mothers when they cry, to be comforted in the Bishop's living quarters. A 'new' dream-born church, yet in essence as old as the hills where runaway slaves sought refuge, its services combine the styles of Jamaican Revival Zionists and Trinidadian Spiritual Baptists. Bishop Noel comes from the island of Grenada, but he has spent a lot of time in Trinidad.

These services last four hours at a time, twice as long as those of the Church of God. Members gather around the centre pole, where a bowl of olive oil is handed around. In turn, hands are dipped into the oil and rubbed. Dreams and revelations are gradually turning Mount Zion more African. Could olive oil be a substitute for palm oil, sacred in some parts of West Africa? According to Bishop Noel, 'Olive oil is good for the health, physical and spiritual, the soul and the spirit and all things.'

Once our hands are oiled, the service proceeds in familiar evangelical fashion. When Bishop Noel opens worship with a hearty cry of 'Greetings to the Household of Faith!', there is no chorused reply, for the chanted responses of the Church of God are absent or altered here. Hymns are sung from the *Redemption Songbook*, with tunes from nineteenth-century England, not Tennessee.

Choruses spring up spontaneously, and have a flavour more traditional than those heard in the Church of God. Instead of Brother Clarendon's modern drumkit, quiet palms patter on conga drums or bongos. The dapper keyboard player sits by the door, and tambourines rattle among the congregation.

Pray, pray, Elisha!
I just want to hear Elisha pray again!

Bishop Noel rings a handbell vigorously, and the voice of Mother Wonder rises above the buzz of prayer, as she addresses a petition of praise and pleas to the Archangels:

'Gabriel, Michael, Rafael, Azrael, hear my prayers!'

Church of God members view this practice dimly, as they believe you should pray only to God and to Jesus. 'Some o' the angel dem may be Fallen, but they still pray to them so', is the usual complaint.

Mount Zion and its sister churches each boast an altar table, laden with items of worship. Candles flicker around a small golden globe vase containing marigolds or primroses. This golden globe orb is called a Lota, and symbolizes the world. Holy water and oil in bottles are lined up beside the great handbell. In the Church of God, only one bottle of olive oil is kept, for anointing the foreheads of members in need of healing. Here, holy water is scattered constantly around the four corners of the church. West Africans place bowls of food or oil for the ancestors around the village tree. Here the bowls around the central pole are full of oil or white wax. A box of chalks is placed nearby.

Chalk pictures and markings, known as 'vévé writing' in New Orleans and Haiti, depict ladders to Heaven, accompanied by laurel trees, prayer wheels and triangular marks whose significance is known only to the robed Mothers and the church hierarchy. These are drawn on the carpet, up the walls and even on the covers of Bibles. The service consists of a Devotional, a Testimony Time, a Healing Call, a Message, an Altar Call and a Closing Prayer and Benediction, not always in that order. Visions, dreams and visitations from the Holy Spirit control the actions of the members.

'We fast for three weeks, only drinking water, and then God speak to us in Visions,' a Mother told me. Not all members fast so drastically, only the elect. Milder fasts, sometimes lasting all night, with music and prayer, are called 'mournings' (or 'mo'nings').

'Candles and bells must be lit and rung only with the guidance of the Holy Spirit,' a typewritten Church Rule proclaims. A sense of Mystery overwhelms me as the service proceeds. Seemingly spontaneous actions have their own rules and method, known apparently to angels and the Holy Spirit. Evergreens, laurel and ivy, sprout from vases and flowerpots. One of the Mothers is named Mother Ivy.

Now Mother Israel gives the announcements: church get-togethers, fasts, feasts, baptisms and 'All Night Tarrying'. She repeats herself carefully, adding '. . . For peradventure, some might mistake the date.'

Only those who have been 'robed', an elaborate ceremony, are entitled to be called Mothers. The splendour and dignity of a Mother needs to be seen to be believed. Nevertheless, when a Mother takes the Devotional Service, her voice is almost drowned at times by an overspill of chorus, 'Come on, children, come on!'

Some members repeat the words softly, others hum. After another song, 'I'm on my way – to Canaan La-and', Testimonies are invited. Members stand to tell the church how they came to find Jesus, and how Jesus has helped them.

'I want to be like an African baby, swaddled and carried on Jesus' back,' a young lady murmurs.

A few hymns and prayers later, the Healing Call is announced. A middle-aged woman goes forward, kneels and whispers her troubles to an attentive Bishop Noel. As he prays loudly over her, another chorus is 'raised', drums whisper and the keyboard organ replies sympathetically. Jesus treated the mentally ill as 'beings possessed', and the Mount Zionists extend this approach to physical ailments. Demons of sickness must be symbolically bound and beaten. Mothers wave slender white wands. Implements of their calling, wands, wooden swords and truncheons covered in strange patterns hang from their belts. No person is ever struck, only the invisible demons suffer, hovering over the afflicted ones. The higher ranks of Mothers are called 'Shepherdesses', and carry tall wooden crooks. Ordinary adult members are described as 'Marys and Josephs'.

Warming to his task, Bishop Noel replaces his green and red turban with a crimson headband, and significantly dons a black necklace of thick tow rope. Loops of ropes are produced and unwound by helpful Mothers. One is stretched before the altar. Praying, humming and bongo-drumming build up and up, until the unwell woman faints. Her arms are then hung over the stretched rope, which balances her, while lesser ropes are tied lightly round and round her body. Blue or scarlet-robed Mothers raise their truncheons and caress the air. Bishop Noel tightens and untightens the woman's bonds a few times, rolls her along the floor and then triumphantly removes the ropes. Everyone crowds forward to see if the woman is healed. Yes, she opens her eyes, gives a weak smile and is helped back to her seat. There she mumbles her thanks and declares herself to be 'much better'.

'Praise the Lord!' booms Bishop Noel. His Message now begins, and we all bend over our Bibles.

'Jesus tells us we must forgive our enemies! Not only forgive, but forget your wrongs if you are to live at peace with the Lord! Forgive and Forget live in the same house . . . .'

An hour goes by, as the Bishop's great voice rises and falls like an ocean swell.

'In dreams, the soul goes on a journey! The outer man sleeps, but the inner man travels. I might be asleep in my bed, but appearing in your dream!'

In the seat ahead of me, a sallow eight-year-old girl with ringlets stares at me with melancholy brown eyes across her mother's shoulder. She is too young to understand the Message and her eyes are filled with soulful boredom. As she fans herself with a Sunday School book, I find myself wishing I could paint a Victorian-style picture of the scene.

Finally, the Message comes to an end, and the Altar Call is announced. All present are 'saved', but three young women and one man kneel before the altar, seeking spiritual gifts. Someone leads off with a wailing chorus song:

> Some sweet day when life is o-over
> Some sweet day I'm going away!

The song soon becomes a hum, 'Za Zee Zee Zoo', with deep-voiced 'Bim Bam a Bams' in the background. Men and women, their faces unmoving masks, rise and dance, jerkily at first, then with increasing fervour. Those who gyrate too wildly are danced back to their seats by a forceful Mother in a purple turban. A tall young Nigerian in a white robe spins like a whirling dervish, crying 'Hullo!' at intervals. Ever in command, the Bishop repeats Bible verses in a sing-song voice. Dancers seize the maypole-ribbon and spin the candle-flaring prayer wheel.

By now, the hums have been reduced to guttural sounds, all to the rhythm of 'Some Sweet Day': 'Na Na Na Non Non'. Kindly Mothers anoint the four kneeling figures with oil, and tie white turbans around the heads of two of the girls, as the rest of the congregation dances. Eventually these girls may be officially robed as Mothers. Truncheons pass to and fro above the kneelers. Overcome, the kneeling man jerks his head back and is calmed by a nearby Mother. Now the Closing Prayer commences, and all dancing ceases.

Those who have room to do so, kneel around the centre pole, holding hands. If my little four-year-old niece is present, she invariably sits on the back of my legs at this point, causing excruciating agony. Then all rise and, still holding hands, raise their arms on high. Everybody in the church must hold somebody's hand, with no weak point in the chain. Only the

Bishop is free to move at will, as he ritually beseeches God and all His angels to 'protect us from wizards, witches and socialism!'

Benediction closes the service, and the eight-year-old girl perks up and looks around with new interest.

'Hello, Mr Man!' she exclaims.

The Celestial Church of Christ

Most of the members of the Celestial Church of Christ (or 'Cele' for short) are Nigerians, Yoruba-speaking people whose customs and background are worlds removed from those of West Indians. Not for them the unspoken air of tragedy that hangs over a people whose ancestors were once enslaved. African churches take a unique direction, Heavenbound no doubt, but very different from Caribbean and English congregations. Here is a brief account of 'Cele' and its services.

Samuel Bilewu Oshoffa (1909–85) is the Founder of this church, ever-present in spirit and able to answer prayers. He was born in what is now the Republic of Benin, but his mother's forebears came from Nigeria, kidnapped by Dahomean warriors. A vision came to the Prophet Oshoffa while he was searching the forests of Benin for ebony. He must return to his ancestral land, Imeko, Ogun State, Nigeria, and found the Celestial Church. And so he did. Today his tomb at Imeko is venerated by thousands.

An angel's eye view of a Celestial Church is necessary, for congregations are large and churches almost cathedral-like. At the far end of the former Anglican church can be found, from left to right, a sandpit replica of a West African holy beach, 'Mercyland', complete with a plastic palm tree, a raised altar and a choir platform occupied by a West African sacred jazz orchestra. (Palm fronds are considered sacred in the traditional Yoruba religion.) The style of the church seems to change dramatically midway through a five-hour service. For the first hour and a half the service is more or less Anglican, with glorious organ music. Then the chairs are collected, the congregation sits on the grey-green fitted carpet, drums ring out, and Africa takes over. Not pagan Africa, but a Christian church with African forms of worship.

A centre-aisle path divides the church – women on the left, men on the right. Many of the songs and frequent Messages are in Yoruba, but as many are in English. Worshippers, for the most part, wear 'soutanes', white robes of French priestly origin. Women wear 'cooks' hats' or shawls, for their heads must be covered. Outside the main hall, shoes are piled in the doorway and men and women have their own dressing rooms. Sometimes they sleep in these rooms at night if told that demonic forces are abroad. Higher-grade worshippers are given the title of 'War Leader', and can be possessed by 'Warrior Angels'. Such angels, led by Holy St Michael, usually have African names. Any connection between these angels and Yoruba gods is indignantly denied by the Pastor, Father Peter (known to his flock as 'Daddy'). Incidentally, Ogun State, where the Prophet Oshoffa lies entombed, is named after a pre-Christian god, Ogun, the West African Woden.

At Father Peter's command, the people pray, kneeling with foreheads on the carpet. The band plays, shrill girl vocalists sway around a microphone, and white-robed figures dance to and fro. Still dancing, they purchase candles for a few pence from a smiling War Leader, and crocodile-dance up the aisle one behind the other, to lay the tallow offerings before Father Peter, God's emissary at the altar. Candles that contain animal-fat are said to represent sacrificial fowl or goats. Bananas, pineapples, oranges and other fruit are carried to God on silver dishes, and divided among church members and their children afterwards. Decorated in blue neon lights, one behind the other, all spelling out the word 'Holy', the altar itself seems to recede into the distance.

Processions of white-clad figures, a line of women and a line of men side by side, continually go to the altar, bending to the rhythm of drums and trumpets. On their return journey, they sway out into the hall facing the main door of the church. Pausing at intervals, the buoyant, cheerful worshippers face, in strict unison, the four corners of the church. These they bless with a threefold chorus of 'Holee!' Everyone then returns to his or her place, and sits comfortably on the floor to hear Father Peter's sermon. When the sermon is over, the processions begin afresh, to layer upon layer of drum rhythm.

Father Peter, the Chief Shepherd, opens his Message by quoting a Yoruba saying: 'Everybody wishes his enemies dead.'

'Why must our people be so obsessed with enemies?' he asks, as well he may. Brooding about enemies is the curse of West Africa.

We say we hate our enemies because they hate us, but this is not the Way of Jesus. Jesus says we must *love* our enemies! There was a rich man who coveted a poor man's beautiful wife! So this rich man goes to a juju man and buys a dangerous medicine. Next day, the rich man seeks out the poor man and offers him the medicine, saying, 'Drink this, it will make you strong!'

Grateful, the poor man takes the medicine home. But meanwhile, the poor man's best friend has had a dream. In this dream, he has seen the poor man drinking medicine and dying in agony. So as soon as he awakens, he runs to the poor man and tells him, just in time.

'Are you sure?' the poor man enquires.

'I am positive! A dream tells the truth, my friend!'

Angrily, the poor man goes to the rich man and accuses him. The rich man confesses everything!

'Now I know you are my enemy!' the poor man tells him.

Aha! What does the poor man do now, but seek out a juju man himself! He asks for a medicine to kill the rich man. Ha, but it is the same juju man, faithful to the rich client who can pay him more!

'Take this potion,' says the juju man, 'and put it under the sand where the rich man walks. But first, step on it yourself!'

As soon as the poor man stamps on the potion, he dies in agony and the rich man gets his wife! The moral is – Love your enemies, and do not seek revenge.

Listening on, I learn that Yoruba have Untouchables, just like Indians.

Did this ever happen to you as a child? A man comes to your door and asks for food. You give him some, but then your mother finds out, and takes a switch to you for a beating you never forget! She has to wash the floor, purify the place, and break all the dishes from which the person ate . . . .

Just as I grow interested, the sermon switches into Yoruba, later repeated in English translation. Father Peter complains that the children are not learning Yoruba or any African language, and says that this will estrange them from their parents in years to come.

A hymn is sung, with rattling calabashes instead of Caribbean tambourines. As the last procession files out, we are met by a man holding a crucifix, who hands out twists of paper containing salt.

'When you get home, sprinkle this on your doorstep and make the sign of the cross over your door,' I am told.

Everyone is very concerned that their fellow members and visitors enjoy immunity from evil spirits.

'You should stay here the night – I think you need protection,' a young lady tells me gravely.

'No, I'm expected at home.'

'I see. My greetings to your children. My greetings to your mother. . . .'

Although the formal service is over, various blessings and benevolent spells are taking place all over the building. Men and women now stroll around together freely, or squat around the slender stone columns that coincidentally resemble Bishop Noel's sacred tree. The large church has been inherited from Anglicans. I overhear a War Leader telling a young lady to take home 'a bottle of holy water and three different kind of fruit, and all will be well'. Another Leader holds a metal chalice of holy water to a child's lips and orders him to drink.

In the music area, site of the former choir, the trumpet player excels himself. Ethereal notes, now Latin, now New Orleans, ride over warm insistent West African drumbeats. Additional rhythm is provided by guitars and by sticks clacked together, the musicians bobbing and weaving in a bunch. Not all the drums are beaten by hand – some young men dance around rapping with hooked wooden or metal drumsticks on hour-glass-shaped Speaking Drums. These drums are carried under one arm, beaten at either end and controlled in tone by a cord around the 'waist'. Yoruba is a tonal language, like Chinese, and subtle cord-loosenings and tightenings control the drums' speech. Sometimes, on a bus, I cannot tell if the talkative people sitting behind me are Chinese or Yoruba.

With a cry of 'Discipline!' a triumphant woman bursts in and chases the children over to the holy seasands of Mercyland, brandishing a stick torn from the hedge outside. Such a cloud of incense hangs over the sandpit that the tall plastic palm and other bright pot plants, real or imitation, loom at me through a heavy mist. Packed into the walled 'beach', with adults pressed around watching, the enchanting, white-clad children are rendered demon or witch-free by having a yellow waist-scarf brushed over their foreheads. A child with a twisted leg is said, by the Leader in charge, to have been bewitched. Candles are dipped in holy water and distributed to the children. Little clumps of burning candles stand in the bright yellow sand, along with bouquets of flowers and holy pictures.

All around the church, adults praying for healing and Special Needs lie stretched out on the floor, beneath sheets, candles burning at their heads and feet. When the candles are burnt out, God will have acknowledged their pleas. In just the same way, medieval monks spent the night of their first monastic vow. In 'Cele', Shepherds and Shepherdesses strike yellow scarfs, important badges of office, over the recumbent figures. One of these figures, evidently in a trance, is my Ibo friend Christopher Osa Ikhinmwin. To my surprise, he raises his head as I leave.

'Goodbye, Roy – see you!' he calls.

CHAPTER THREE

The Brotherhood of the Cross and Star

Behold Him who is now revealed,
Health, peace, life for man.
His glory fills Heaven and earth;
Olumba Olumba Obu!

Father, great Olumba,
Giver of what is good;
Keep us in Brotherhood
Till we see the promised day.

Olumba Olumba Obu

At first sight, the Brotherhood of the Cross and Star seems a typical West African Spiritual Church. Members wear white robes, offer fruit to all and sundry, and dance along in line to the altar. True, they believe instrumental music to be sinful, and accompany hymns with hummed mouth-music ('Nnn nnn nnn'), but this is a minor detail. The startling fact about the Brotherhood of the Cross and Star is that most members believe their leader, Olumba Olumba Obu, to be the reincarnated Messiah.

Unlike Jamaican Rastafarians who regard themselves as non-Christian (and therefore outside the scope of this book), Brotherhood believers regard themselves as belonging to a Christian church. Rastafarians may worship the late Emperor of Ethiopia, Haile Selassie, as God, and the Brotherhood worship their elderly leader, Olumba Olumba Obu. There is an ever-present temptation in mankind to deify and then worship a leader. Nigerians seem particularly prey to this weakness at this time, though I admit that as a boy in the 1940s I myself was encouraged to worship Stalin. The Yoruba Celestial Church of Christ stops just short of claiming their Founder, the Prophet Oshoffa, to be completely omnipotent.

Olumba Olumba Obu lives near the banks of the River Biakpan ('the new Jordan') at Calabar, not far from the border between Nigeria and Cameroon. Many of his followers are members of the Efik tribe, others are Ibos and Ibibios. O.O.O. himself speaks Efik and the unique Biakpan language. According to a Brotherhood tract:

The Universal Landlord is Here! In 1918, the Supreme Spirit of Creator God Almighty was born into this world as human. His mission this time is to establish the Kingdom of God on this earth, and to rule the universe with Love, Peace, Mercy, Power, Goodwill, Imagination, Zeal, Strength, Order, Wisdom, Etc. The Entire Universe must be informed, before the Year 2000, that all those who do not Recognize O.O.O. as God and Leader of the New Earth in human form will be destroyed.

Such a message seems irresistible to many white English people who are attracted to this church alone, out of all the great variety of West African Spiritual Churches. In Birmingham, Moss Side in Manchester and Toxteth in Liverpool, the Brotherhood of the Cross and Star has a unifying effect in its church (or Bethel) neighbourhoods. Despite the frightening note in the tract just quoted, Brotherhood pastors preach the Christian virtues, although with scant mention of Original Sin. Optimism is a feature of Brotherhood sermons and testimonies.

I well remember the testimonies of Ibo members at the Toxteth (Liverpool Eight) Bethel of the Brotherhood. This church, to my mind, has done as much for good neighbourliness and true brotherhood in Liverpool as have the two nearby Anglican and Catholic cathedrals put together. Whether it should be regarded as a Christian church is a matter of opinion.

Liverpool's Bethel of the Brotherhood of the Cross and Star is held in an imposing Gothic church whose spire dominates that corner of Toxteth where the 1980s riots hit the hardest. Here, at the juncture of Upper Parliament Street and Prince's Boulevard, a hospital for the elderly was set on fire, the patients rescued just in time. A bank and several other buildings were torched, but the Brotherhood was spared.

At Testimony Time (when members get up to speak of spiritual experiences) a girl with a strong Liverpool accent told the congregation that she had used a swearword that week, but had at once apologized to Olumba.

Finally, a stately, dark-skinned young lady in a white robe stood up and proclaimed:

We are mostly Ibos, of the Ibo Nation. There is a Kingdom of Heaven and a Kingdom of Hell on earth. England is a United Kingdom. It is the Kingdom of Heaven! If we work, we have food. If we do not work, we can still have food. If we decide to stop working before we are very old, someone will look after us. This is also what it is like in the Kingdom of Heaven.

We have all read about people like Christopher Columbus and Mungo Park. These good people came from these parts of the world and travelled long distances to bring wealth to their countries. Others reap what they have sowed. I wonder who Mrs Thatcher was in her previous life? She must have been somebody good, to be so rewarded!

At that time, Mrs Thatcher was in the final year of her premiership. Quite apart from the avowed belief in reincarnation, traditional to West Africa, this Testimony is remarkable for containing the only kind word about Mrs Thatcher that I have ever heard spoken in Liverpool!

'Oh, Sweet Mother-O'

In July 1991 the Brotherhood of the Cross and Star held an enormous outdoor Convention in Trafalgar Square. Posters on the Underground advertised the event, and showed the smiling face of Olumba Olumba Obu, the Leader declared a Messiah by his followers. Olumba himself denies that he is Christ, or God, but his followers just think he's being modest. So he lets it slide.

It was a bright sunny day, and the whole square seemed agleam with white robes and cooks' hats. True, the Brotherhood had not climbed Nelson's Column, but they had raised a platform high on its base, and also cordoned off a large area, lined with chairs.

'Peace!' somebody greeted me, and I recognized my London neighbour, Deaconess Leung, a fervent Malay-Chinese member of the church.

In breathless excitement, she told me that although O.O.O. could not attend this meeting of the Bethels, the Holy Queen Mother would be the honoured guest. Helen Obu, the Holy Queen, was not Olumba's actual mother or wife, but his daughter. She was also, I seemed to understand, the reincarnation of her Holy grandmother.

Before descending to the square, I tried to interest the Anti-Apartheid protesters outside South Africa House in the event.

'We are not interested in everything that Africans do, but only in ending apartheid,' a leafleting schoolboy told me. So clutching African leaflets of every kind, I joined the Olumba-worshippers around the lions.

Pigeon-feeding families and tourists seemed delighted to find Olumba-ites in their midst, and the square was full of smiles. In the cordoned-off sector, a throne had been prepared for the Holy Mother, a big chair draped in lace. A carpet edged with flowers led to the holy seat. Conventioneers buzzed around, uttering their 'Nna nn' mouth music.

'Hallelujah!' cried a tall Deaconess from the platform.

'We can't hear you!' several voices replied.

Turning up her megaphone, the Deaconess told us that this was 'not a church, but God's Kingdom on Earth!' As she preached her message of love and brotherhood, I roamed around looking at the Convention-goers. Women outnumbered men by four to one. Some wore cream-coloured robes, but most wore brilliant white, often with scarlet sashes. White is a traditional colour of holiness and purity in West Africa as in most other countries. Below the classical columns of the National Gallery, young English members of the church resembled Romans in togas and bare feet.

Two of these young men were the sons of Bishop Jeremy Goring, a revered Brotherhood leader who lives at Lewes, Sussex. A gentle, white-haired man, with startling black eyebrows, the Bishop used to be Dean of

Humanities at Goldsmiths' College, London. He is now an honorary Chief of Biakpan, a place which, he tells me, is both magical and astonishingly like the Sussex Weald. In addition to being a retired scholar, Dr Goring is a Unitarian minister in Lewes. His sons are 'Servants of God', rather like monks, and cannot marry.

Suddenly I noticed a car, wreathed wedding-style in red roses and scarlet streamers. It was already empty. The Holy Queen Mother had arrived! Looking around, I saw a big, thick-set, stern woman stamping righteously along like a Care Attendant in a home for frail old people, holding up a large yellow-and-red striped umbrella. For a moment, I thought she must be the Holy Queen herself, a fearsome monarch. Then I looked beneath the brolly, West African symbol of Royalty, and saw a modest, thin, bespectacled woman walking diffidently towards her throne, with downcast eyes. This was the real Holy Queen. She was dressed as a bride, a leaf pattern on her white robes.

Once seated on her throne, she took no part in the preaching and humming, but modestly and silently accepted the veneration of the crowd.

> 'Oh, sweet Mother-O!
> You are the reigning Queen!'

sang the Sabbath Choir.

A conga line of mischievous, white-clad children paraded out and collected money from the faithful and passers-by alike. Many of the Brotherhood kneeled with foreheads on the ground, facing the Queen. Others made obeisance to a silver dish of flowers, that may have symbolized Olumba. Those who danced clasped their hands in prayer, releasing them to drop money into the children's bags. Dancers, mainly women, doubled up and undoubled, weaved, bobbed and waved their arms, chanting and ululating.

Moss Side Bethel

Joy, joy! Heaven is full of
Joy, joy! Come one by one!

Eventually the Holy Queen had to leave, escorted by the choir and shaded by the umbrella. A demure wave from the car window and she was gone. At once, both song and dance became more frenetic, and all Trafalgar Square seemed a bobbing mass of white, the Farewell dance:

On your way, Olumba, I go!

'The Holy Queen Mother is like the Virgin Mary,' a tall worshipper informed a pigeon-feeder.

Now came the Blessing as the rear doors of white vans were opened to reveal mountains of fresh fruit. Smiling Deaconesses danced around the Square holding trays laden with sliced water melons, oranges and apples, bunches of grapes and chopped bananas. Each type of fruit had its separate tray, offered to all. Near a green fountain that sprayed droplets over the dancers, I found Deaconess Leung in charge of the oranges. She smiled an Olumba farewell, and I left the square, licking fruit juice from my fingers.

Moss Side Bethel

Almost two years later, a Reception for Jeremy Goring was held at the Bethel (church) of the Brotherhood of the Cross and Star at Moss Side, Manchester. I had heard frightening tales of Moss Side, but found the reality of narrow, parallel rows of red-brick doll's house terraces cosy and reassuring. Children played merrily in the streets, but the back alleys were neglected and full of dustbin bags. Each strip of terrace had two slate roofs, a top roof and a continuous alcove roof above the ground floor windows. Flocks of magpies swooped noisily from tree to tree and out into the greenery of Alexandra Park. Although it was my first visit, my mother had lived here as a small girl in the 1920s.

'Spiritual School for Practical Christianity', a huge sign proclaimed from the end wall of a long, low brick building. I slipped off my shoes in the hall and entered the Bethel. Arriving too late to meet the Bishop, I was nevertheless made welcome, and sat facing an altar decorated with a picture of Olumba. Above his portrait this message was emblazoned in scarlet neon lettering: 'Leader O.O.O., the Sole Spiritual Head.' White frilly curtains hung over the doors, for the Bethel contained several rooms, including a kitchen and a bathroom. West Africans like to live in their churches. Bunting hung from the ceiling, along with large placards marking out areas of the church – 'Men's Congregation', 'Women's Congregation' and 'Ordained Students'.

Brother Treasure Edemikoh welcomed me, and the atmosphere was friendly and relaxing. Pastor Obi was giving a talk on church songs.

'Many are in ethnic languages we do not fully understand,' he explained, 'so in future let us sing in English.'

'What does he mean?' I asked Brother Treasure.

'I am an Ibibio,' Brother Treasure replied, in the usual shy embarrassment brought on by mention of tribes. 'The group of villages in Biakpan are in Efik country, and many of the songs are in Efik. But in England, few members are Efik. Biakpan's twelve villages are the home of the Biakpan people – they speak and of course sing in Biakpan, which I cannot. It is to these people that our Leader was born.'

Long ago, I thought I had made a great breakthrough in my knowledge of Africa when I realized that the nation states shown in atlases are new and still somewhat artificial boundaries drawn upon Africa by white people. The *real* African peoples, I thought, are divided into tribes – Ibos, Ibibios, Yorubas and so on. But now I realise that I can *never* untangle Africa's secrets, for the tribes all have clans, often distinguished by totem animals. Clans, or tribes within the tribes, are normally centred on groups of nine to twelve villages, and command more loyalty than do tribes.

Within each straggling village of the clan group are different *wards*, each with its proud history, resentful of rivals. There, a box within a box, can be found the prominent local families! And then – but no, I give up! Biakpan appears to be a unique miniature nation surrounded on all sides by the friendly Efik tribe.

A jolly Pickwickian man, with the face of a cherub in spectacles, Pastor Obi ended his talk and called for prayer. Most of the church prayed kneeling with foreheads on the floor. The children, a high-spirited bunch of white-robed infants, took this as an opportunity to crawl in train-like lines, single file, in and out of the pews, across the aisle with its deep blue carpet and around the whole Bethel on hands and knees. Adults smiled at them indulgently. I remembered that in the Celestial Church of Christ the Yoruba children were gently treated by Nigerian standards.

I remember listening with sympathy as a Nigerian once told me how much he had hated polishing the family shoes each morning, his allocated child's task. Just then he noticed a speck of dust on his own shoe, and roared an order to his tiny nephew who rushed in with a cloth and began to polish, quivering with fear. It was his allocated task. Back in Hausa-land, north Nigeria, children kneel before their parents, silently awaiting orders. Their suffering is mitigated by the thought that one day they will be adult and able to make their *own* children, nephews or child-slaves suffer.

A good-humoured statuesque lady, Elizabeth Maduka, brought me food and drink. Brother Treasure gave me Olumba-pamphlets, and from these I learned that kindness to children is a deliberate Cross and Star policy.

'Very many children', one tract-writer observed, 'as soon as they hear the voices of their parents want to vanish because of fear. Some of them quake at the sight of their parents. Even a person who is not capable of fighting his equal will always wage war against his children at home. . . .'

Nine pages were devoted to an impassioned plea for kindness to children, with copious quotations from the words of Jesus. Fathers were reminded of the old days in West Africa, when twins and their mothers were sometimes put to death. That custom had ended, so why not other customs?

So the Brotherhood of the Cross and Star, I thought to myself, are helping to undo a great social evil. It is in towns such as Lagos, Calabar or Manchester that West African family life can be at its most fraught. West Indians and most English people believe that traditional village Africans 'live in huts'. So they do, but not all squashed into *one* hut. Each household consists of several huts within a large family compound. The compound is the equivalent of a big airy house, and the huts are *rooms*, one for each person. Scampering around such a compound, a small child can easily avoid oppressive relatives and tag along after kind-hearted favourites. When squashed into one flat or room in Western fashion, many families could do with spiritual guidance.

Olumba Olumba Obu, I read, had been born in 1918, the year of the great 'flu epidemic. No doubt engendered by the Great War, the world-wide epidemic killed more people than its parent had done, and spread to remote African villages where Europe and its problems were unknown. Influenza Gods joined Smallpox Gods as illness personified and dangerous deities to be propitiated. Olumba's birth, at a time when other children were dying, took on great significance. In one of his aspects, Olumba Olumba Obu is a 'Healing Messiah'. He is apparently an accomplished faith healer.

Unlike the spiritual leaders of antiquity, O.O.O. has a permanent address: 3, Ambo Street, Calabar, Nigeria. If you want to know more about the Brotherhood of the Cross and Star, you can write to him yourself.

Waving goodbye to friendly Pastor Obi, Brother Treasure, Sister Elizabeth Maduka and other West Africans, I crossed the road to the

Jamaican Church of God. There I learned that a successful District Convention had come to an end. Moss Side may be a place where shops have barred windows and padlocked gates across their doorways, but there is no shortage of Houses of God.

The Brotherhood of the Cross and Star

This extraordinary and picturesque church originated in the Biakpan region of eastern Nigeria. Biakpanites and Efik tribesmen form the inner circles of membership, together with Ibos, Ibibios and all tribes westward to Lewes, Sussex. In England, white membership is growing.

A Deaconess Day (*opposite*) in a Bethel (church) of the Brotherhood of the Cross and Star, at Elephant and Castle in London. A portrait of Olumba Olumba Obu, the quasi-divine church founder, looks down upon his faithful followers. He is believed to be the eighth and final reincarnation of the godhead. Pictures of 'O.O.O.' (as the Leader is known) adorn the flags on high, beneath which members walk in slow procession to the low altar to receive a blessing and to give an offering.

'Olumba is the Light!' The serenity of Moss Side, Manchester, is disturbed by the sudden joyous appearance of members of the Brotherhood of the Cross and Star on an 'Outing', or outdoor crusade. The occasion celebrates the nineteenth anniversary of the Brotherhood in Britain.

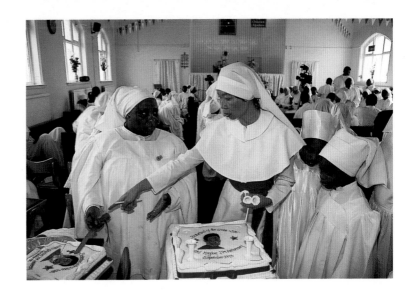

Deaconess Leung (*above right*) cuts the Anniversary Cake, adorned with a picture of the Leader, in the Bethel at Moss Side.

Children file towards the altar (*right*) to receive a blessing and to give offerings. A coin pressed between praying hands is dropped reverently into a glass vase.

Silent prayer at the all-night vigil in Manchester contrasts with the spiritual dancing (*opposite*); the vigorous gestures imitate those of the preacher, who at this moment embodies the Founder, O.O.O.

Deaconess Rosemary and Bishop Jeremy Goring (from Lewes in Sussex) preside over the anniversary celebrations (*above*). Founder Olumba personally appointed Bishop Goring as his representative in western Europe.

These three pictures show a House Blessing conducted by Brother Henshaw in a member's flat in Brixton, London. Each room is sanctified by a sprinkling of holy water, a service is held with a table as improvised altar, after which everyone sits down to a House Feast eaten solemnly in remembrance of our Lord.

Overleaf: **In Covent Garden, London**, where once the Romano-British goddess Coventina was worshipped, Olumba Olumba Obu is venerated in song and dance by the Central Choir of the Brotherhood of the Cross and Star. Instrumental music is considered sinful by the Brotherhood. As in Wales, choral singing is encouraged.

CHAPTER FOUR

The Water Is Troubled

I've been to the water, and I've been baptized.
My soul got happy and I'm satisfied!

(SONG HEARD IN THE CHURCH OF GOD)

The washing away of sin is a symbolism easily understood. West African worship of the ocean may have prompted the Mount Zionists to choose the sea as God's baptismal tank. In the more orthodox Church of God a tank is used for the candidates' Big Day, and the ceremony follows that of any Baptist Church, except for the music.

To a soulful, quavering chant, 'The Water Is Troubled, My Friend, Step Right In', the convert succumbs to the heated waters, and is swished under and out by an adept Pastor and Deacon. If a man, he will wear ordinary clothes; if a woman, a white robe and a matching bathing cap. A spare outfit, brought in a bag, awaits the new dripping wet Brother or Sister. With raised hand, the convert stands waist deep in the tank for several minutes, along with Pastor and Deacon, as prayers and promises are loudly uttered. Drums, claves (or hitting sticks), guitars and tambourines are played, and urgent 'hellfire preaching' leads on to an Altar Call.

Child-christenings are not held in any of the churches I describe. Babies are dedicated to Jesus in short prayerful ceremonies in the Church of God and at Mount Zion, in the hope that they will attend church in later life, but no water baptism takes place. Fashionable young parents, distinguished from church members by their gold-ringed dandiness, often bring their babies along on Sundays to be blessed. All the church loves a baby, and cameras flash from every angle.

Mount Zion Baptism

My good friend Evangelist Hilda Steadman from Jamaica makes an imposing sight as she sails with stately mien around the East End of London, Handsworth in Birmingham, Salford and occasionally Chicago, handing out tracts with the promise of Redemption wheresoever she goes. Her turban and blue and gold gown have become a legend, her flat at Stratford East a place of frequent prayer meetings.

Many years ago, so the Evangelist tells me, her Special Calling was noted by none other than Bishop Noel, in the days when he worked as a traffic warden. A stranger to her at the time, he stopped her in the street on an impulse and declared that she was a holy woman. Intrigued, Mrs Steadman attended Mount Zion until her Calling drew her further afield.

One room of her over-furnished council flat has been set aside for prayer, with a row of chairs facing a makeshift altar on which an open Bible rests. A photograph of her adopted daughter Precious has been placed upon the Book. On the walls hang paintings of fruit and flowers, together with closely written texts in the Evangelist's artistic hand. In the hall, above eye-level, hangs a shelf-like shrine with candles, figurines, olive oil and a photograph of the Evangelist herself. A large wooden cross leans in one corner.

Longing to see her old friend Bishop Noel once more, Evangelist Steadman agreed to come with me on the Mount Zion coach trip to the seaside for the annual sea baptism. This occurs every August at a chosen South Coast resort. When blessed by Bishop Noel, the Channel becomes an honorary River Jordan. All the 'Mount' family of churches attend, meeting at a prearranged spot where coaches from Oxford, Slough and Huddersfield may park.

At seven in the morning, the Evangelist knocked at my door, and we made our way down the road to Mount Zion Spiritual Baptist Church.

There we found the drums rocking and the congregation 'dancing in the spirit', their bodies bending and arms moving like pistons. Mount Zion Nurses tended the five young women candidates for baptism, who were robed in white with head cloths and blindfolds to match. They had been ritually blindfolded on the previous evening, had stayed up in church all night, and would not be allowed to see until waist-deep in Jordan Stream. Mothers and Shepherds busied themselves gathering tall, heavy staffs, crosses and other items.

Bishop Noel and Evangelist Steadman greeted one another, the Bishop's booming-voiced flamboyance contrasting with the matronly Evangelist's air of soft-spoken tragedy. Leaving the Bishop anxiously scanning the horizon for hired coaches, the Evangelist and I took our seats in the crowded church. Before long, my friend raised her eerily sanctified Bessie Smith voice in song with the others.

> Don't ever trouble Zion!
> Don't ever trouble Zion!
> Zion have a gift to open sinners' hearts,
> So don't ever trouble Zion!

Shadows from two coaches outside fell across Mount Zion, and soon we were in our seats and bowling along the highway. To the Evangelist's mild chagrin, we found ourselves in the *secular* coach, reserved for those who were not full members, such as 'visiting friends' and children. All the singing and ecstasy was going on in the coach ahead of us. There Bishop Noel presided over the fully robed and rollicking Mothers, who danced up and down the coach, heard but not seen by the five blindfolded candidates, each of whom sat holding a burning candle.

Feeling left out, the unrobed woman beside us started backbiting. 'There's no love in this church, no love at all,' she complained. 'I only goes 'cos my brother belong here.'

Ignoring this slur, Evangelist Steadman briskly organized chorus-singing, and soon a happier atmosphere prevailed. The songs, however, like 'Don't Trouble Zion', were slow, mournful and poignant.

Road, road, road – go down that lonesome road!

During an interval between songs, a young Mount Zionist with a haunted expression told me how much she was looking forward to seeing the baptism. By her speech it was obvious that she had been born and brought up in London.

'The candidates have been dancing and fasting for three days now. Soon they will see Visions. Now we can learn from them about our past and our future. Usually they has visions while they in the sea itself.'

At half-time, when we stopped at a wayside café, Evangelist Steadman prevailed on the Bishop to allow us to ride in the first coach with the robed dancers and candidates. He agreed readily, although our former coach-mates seemed sorry and puzzled to see us go.

'Evangelist Steadman is an old friend of Bishop Noel from a long time,' I explained.

Now we rolled on in gaudy, musical, candle-lit triumph to the majestic tones of 'Roll, Jordan, Roll' and other spirituals. Before long we encountered three more 'Mount' coaches from the provinces, all heading through open countryside to the same resort. The Evangelist looked through her bag, which contained empty bottles to be filled with holy sea-water, and boxes for seaweed.

Bishop Noel greeted the pastors from the other churches, and nodded benignly as the blindfolded candidates were led hesitatingly down from coach steps to the tarmac. Women wore white blindfolds, men red. Before long we were marching in procession to the shingly beach, those in the rear struggling with an altar table. Holidaymakers seemed less surprised than I had expected.

The altar table was set down on a flat stretch of beach, well above high water mark, and nearly everybody gathered around it for a lengthy service, complete with Bible references and Redemption hymns. Candles, flowers, bells, Lotas and bottles were arranged on the table in familiar order. While a Mother took the service, Bishop Noel and the Bishop from Slough busied themselves planting staffs and crosses at strategic points. One staff and cross were placed in the sand, several yards apart, and another two were carried far out to sea. The two Bishops walked boldly into the Jordan until waves washed over their shoulders. Making sure that the two tall poles were well secured in the sea bed, yet clearly visible above the surface, the men rejoined the Mothers at the altar.

Preaching with vigour, a powerfully-built, high-turbaned Mother sang out words of holiness in an impressive chanting voice, perhaps inspired by Anglican responses, but now sounding slow, impressive and mysteriously African. She based her sermon on the Life of St Paul, who was blinded and restored to sight. Then she spoke of John the Baptist and of the wonderful baptism of Jesus.

'I say to *you*, Mount Zion, you must be*lieve*, O Mount Zion!' she chanted.

'True! If you go in the water a sinner, you emerge a wet sinner,' a nearby Mother remarked.

At last the time of immersion drew near, Bishop Noel rang his bell furiously, and the imposing Mother led the candidates (aided by Nurses) to the shore. As she did so, she sang in a commanding voice, over and over:

> I see the river, I see the pool,
> I can see the river where John baptize!
> John baptize and I baptize!
> I can see the river where John baptize!

The first two phrases were sung in a series of drawn out wails, akin to a blues song, while the 'I can see the river' line hurried along in rhythmic calypso fashion. So did the candidates hurry along. By now, Bishop Noel and his fellow Bishop awaited them at the furthermost cross and staff, way out at sea. Each unsteady, blindfolded figure was baptized not once but three times, with great ringing of bells. One girl refused to let go of her candle, long blown out by sea breezes, and only threw it away when her time came to go under. Another girl candidate struggled in Bishop Noel's arms, yet when her baptism was over and her blindfold carefully unwrapped, she danced for joy in the waves, arms held on high.

All this while, Evangelist Steadman had been searching for seaweed. Children who had come along with their parents on the coach were quickly enlisted in the cause, delightedly snatching up olive-green strands of stringy weed from among the stones and giving them to the Evangelist in return for a few pence. She also collected unusual shells and ocean-polished pebbles.

'Back home in Jamaica, I always make Irish Moss', she said. 'When I boil it, it does turn to jelly, you know. It a cure for all kind of ailment.'

'Maybe English seaweed is different,' the haunted-looking young girl suggested, but the Evangelist doubted it.

Once she had collected her seaweed, the Evangelist turned her attention to holy water, and took several empty plastic bottles from her bag. At the shore, she asked a startled white boy who was paddling with his sister, to fill them for her. He did so eagerly.

'You should get the water after the baptisms, when Bishop Noel blesses the sea,' the helpful London-born girl told Evangelist Steadman. 'It might not be holy water yet.'

'Yes, yes, him does bless the sea before he begin to baptize, as well,' the Evangelist said equably. 'When I gets home, I shall soak my corns!'

Out at sea, the baptisms over, the Bishops and Mothers held hands in a circle and danced a prayer in the waves. Then, in full costume, both Bishops threw themselves forward and swam powerfully, using a dog stroke and blowing like grampuses. Soaked all over, Bishop Noel staggered ashore and beamed at me.

'Now I'm going to fast for seven days!' he announced. 'That's the way to see things!'

Visions had to wait, as he had to preach a winding-up service after a change of clothes. Newly-dried candidates were made to drink sea water, using the Bishop's bell as a chalice. Local people and holidaymakers gathered around, friendly and curious.

'Are you Moslems?' a stout lady in a swimsuit enquired, misled by the Arab-like robes of Mount Zion.

'No, we're Baptists,' came the reply, to her incredulity. Mount Zionists seemed very different from the usual Baptist Sunday Schools on their seaside outings.

A tough-looking old man turned to me fiercely, as if daring contradiction.

'These are the finest, happiest people you could ever hope to meet! They come here every four years or so, and when they go, they don't leave even a pin behind! Our lot leave the beach looking like a tip! And I've been living in this town for eighty years, so don't you think I have the right to have an opinion?'

Hastily, I agreed, then hurried to meet Evangelist Steadman's call.

'Brother Roy, you think you can buy me an ice cream? I does prefer vanilla, you know.'

His day's work done, Bishop Noel sank into a deckchair and fell sound asleep.

Yoruba Naming Ceremony

From what I hear, prayer ceremonies held on beaches, near the sea, by the Nigerian Celestial Church of Christ somewhat resemble Mount Zion baptisms in spirit. Naming ceremonies for babies, however, have no obvious Caribbean counterpart. Names are very important to most West African people, and a nation or an individual with a new name is believed to be made new, or 'born again'. Among the Yoruba people who form the mainstay of 'Cele', there is a tradition that unnamed babies may more easily become possessed and then killed by poltergeist-like child spirits. Known as Abukis, these spirits live among trees in a haunted spot on the outskirts of a village. Encountering them can be very dangerous, and sometimes leads to death.

Mrs Brown, a friend of mine from a village in Jamaica's Blue Mountains, told me about the haunted grove where 'Abners' played by twilight, the spirits of babies who had died before being named in baptism. Meeting the Abners could prove fatal. Her village had never converted to the Church of God, and the people still worshipped in orthodox English-style churches. Infant baptism was still practised, and so an echo of the Yoruba belief in Abukis remained.

On the night of a naming ceremony, I stood at the back of the 'Men's Side' in the Celestial Church of Christ, jigging to the music of the sacred jazz band. Christmas-style decorations hung everywhere, although it was August. I did not have on the 'soutane' that Mrs Akintola, the church seamstress, had kindly run up for me on her sewing machine. As a wearer of 'mufti', I was barred from entering the more sacred areas of the church. Luckily, I could see fairly well from where I stood. All the chairs had been stacked up, leaving a wide open space for holy dancing.

In the middle of the centre aisle, a small altar table had been placed, where seven candles burned in a bowl of water. Seated at this table, a man in a white robe stared dreamily into space. Suddenly I noticed that he was holding a tiny baby with fluffy hair and half-shut eyes. His wife would not be permitted to enter the church until forty days after giving birth. Seven elders stood at hand, to represent seven hosts of angels. Between the father and the preacher's rostrum, a most enormous, varied and brightly-coloured heap of fruit had been placed. Everyone in the church seemed to have brought along the contents of a fruiterer's shop. Bananas, pears, grapes, apples, oranges and coconuts had been laid out in the shape of a giant man lying on his back. Drums thudded, trumpets and bells rang, as Father Peter, the Chief Shepherd, loudly proclaimed the Yoruba names of the baby boy. These names had not been chosen by the parents – they had been revealed by angels to a Prophetess, and noted down by the church scribe. Dipping his finger into a dish of syrup and sugar, Father Peter placed the sweetness on the baby's lips and intoned 'May your life never be sour!' Then he handed the baby to a severe-looking Prophetess.

Only now had the child become a full member of its own family and the wider family of the church. Pensive no longer, the father's face broke into a wide-eyed smile of pride and wonderment. This was a great day. The Prophetess described the angels she had met: 'They looked like white light, or fire.' She assured everybody that the father had been 'sanctified' (or purified) before and after the names had been announced.

Yoruba chants and prayers filled the church, and I heard the Prophetess refer in English to the baby's circumcision. A dish of burning oil was placed near the door, and a song was raised from the blue *Spiritual Songbook*: 'Shame upon you, Satan!' From the bandstand, a saxophone wailed and someone played a guitar in a style reminiscent of B.B. King.

'Soon we will dance round the baby!' the Prophetess proclaimed, delivering the child to the outstretched arms of a shepherdess. 'In Nigeria, we would offer a ram or a goat in sacrifice, and soon the civilized nations will catch up with us.'

At a given signal, everyone in the church fell on the symbolic fruit pile, children to the fore, and began to eat. The happy father sat on the floor with his baby and enjoyed the picnic. As for me, I went home with a coconut.

CHAPTER FIVE

A Wedding and a Funeral

When the Church of God arises with her garment bright and fair
And ascends to meet the bridegroom for the marriage in the air,
She'll outshine the sun at noonday, not a wrinkle, not a spot.
Will you be among the bride or will you not?

She'll be shining through the ages
After earth and time has been forgotten.
She'll be wearing garments pure and spotless;
Have you on the wedding robe or have you not?

The Wedding

It was a great day at the Mount Zion Spiritual Baptist Church when Teacher Jackie married the neat young pastor of a brother church. Guests and workmates of the couple, some of them white, swelled the usual number of worshippers. Twelve bridesmaids, dressed in pink or pale blue, eyed the door expectantly, for the bride was late. About their brows, they wore wreaths of dried flowers. Blue and yellow paper decorations hung from the ceiling. As for Bishop Noel and his wife, both were gorgeously attired, one in a huge gold bishop's hat, the other in a scarlet-painted royal crown. Half-hidden amongst all this finery, the town hall Registrar impassively awaited events.

Teacher Jackie the bride made a sensational entrance, a mass of white with a fifteen-foot gold train behind. Holding the Cloth of Gold was a tiny girl, dressed in a mass of pink ruffles. The groom, by contrast, wore a black suit and a scarlet bow tie. He was a nervous bespectacled man. Beaming, the bride made her way to the altar on the arm of her brother.

Bishop Noel began the ceremony with a sternness and rigour that would have done credit to St Paul. But as time went by his sense of humour got the better of him, and he ad-libbed his way through the wedding in fine form. Here are some highlights, spoken in a deep, throaty 'gospel voice'.

Now the groom is wishing he could get away, but the crowds are pressed too close!
But why should he run away when his wife's so beautiful, he'd be mad,

innit? . . . Now, groom, press the ring down firm on her finger, we do not want a divorce! You know, whoever pushes the ring furthest down is going to be the ruler! Better push it down together . . . When men see the woman's ring, they stop trying! Or maybe they don't . . . Now wife, be stern unto your husband – he needs it! Yet don't jump to conclusions. If he's out late, don't at once think it's another woman, there might be a good reason . . . Groom, if you don't say 'Yes' at this stage, I'll box your ears! And the bride too – I'll box *her* ears! Lord, guard them from all witchcraft, voodoo, black magic, scientists and socialism, Amen.'

All this while, a hired camcorder man in a black and yellow zebra-patterned suit hopped around trying to film the event. A woman guest shrieked at her child who was playing outside the church, and this so upset her brother, a reluctant churchgoer, that the young man stormed from the building. Nothing could mar the great day, however, and we soon crossed the road to the Community Centre for the Reception.

Here a champagne buffet had been laid on, and we feasted royally on rhoti, a meat-and-chapati dish introduced to the Caribbean by Indian indentured labourers. There were speeches galore, and the bride embarrassed her new husband by saying, 'He kept asking me to marry him!'

Two rows of bridesmaids held bouquets aloft, forming an archway through which the bride and groom slowly waltzed to taped gospel music, seraphic expressions on their faces. Seizing a bouquet, the bride tossed it to an unarmed bridesmaid. Then the serious business of cake-cutting began.

The Funeral

In her little, dark, East End flat I found the Evangelist Steadman to be in a sombre mood. She was not dressed to match her mood, for she wore golden robes beneath a scarlet shawl and turban. But her words were full of omens. In order to cheer up her flat, where water streamed down the walls and cockroaches danced the night away, I had bought her a purplish potted plant in Stratford market.

'I am so pleased with that big-leaf plant,' she told me. 'It is a Croton, an' in Jamaica it grow as big as a tree. Back home, we uses the leaf for funeral wreath. But I am thinking there will be a funeral soon, Brother Roy.'

'Why is that?'

'Some time ago, I hear a knocking at me window pane. It a white dove knocking – somebody dies. Last week I was hill [ill] with neuralgia, I hear a bang by my side. The pain gone, and I know a soul has passed. Last night I dream I see a wooden house hung all over with meat for sale. White meat like pork – that's nothing but a funeral!'

She spoke on, about a 'vigion' (vision) she had seen of a white girl kneeling in her room.

'She look nice, so I was not afraid . . .'

'Are you talking about a dream or something real?' I asked in puzzlement after a while.

'Is a *dream*, me tell you!' she spoke emphatically, her tone suggesting that dreams are real in a way the waking world can never be. Such an attitude is held in all the churches I describe. In Jamaica marriages take place in the Church of God if somebody dreams they saw Brother and Sister so-and-so getting wed. In England, dreams of marriages are often taken as prophecies, as are dreams that portend death. Is Heaven itself a never-ending happy dream we all can share?

A non-church-going Jamaican friend of mine claims he can tell dreams that are visions from dreams that are just dreams. Acting on the former kind of dream, he rushed from London to 'Birningham' in time to call an ambulance for his ailing wife. I took the Evangelist's dreams to heart, and found that she wasn't wrong.

Pastor Spring is, in most ways, a model of everything a pastor should be. In winter, he goes to church at crack of dawn to light the paraffin fires so that members will enter a warm building. Always he impresses on his charges the need to love, respect and cherish old people. Most of them need no telling, for such attitudes are deeply instilled, even in the youngest. Oldest man in the church for some time was Brother Pullman, a tall, frail ninety-year-old. I had to listen to him carefully, for he spoke in deep 'patois'. He had never been to England before this lengthy visit. Pet of the church, to his obvious pleasure, he continued to write to the Brethren after his return to Jamaica.

His first letter caused some embarrassment to young Sister Dorothy who tried to read it to the Congregation.

'It's all written in Jamaican talk,' she appealed to the Pastor, who took over.

'Me feel like a pig with leg tied for market,' the Pastor read. 'Me struggle, but me can't go back to England.'

Everybody clapped when Pastor Spring had finished reading. After reminding the church once more of their duty to love and respect the old, the pastor mentioned the other side of the coin.

'Back home, as many brethren can tell you, grown-up men with wives and children still fear they parents an' get a lickin' from they Mum or Dad.'

Many an outwardly worldly and fashionable Jamaican in England refers to his Mum as 'Mummy' in awe and timidity.

With Brother Pullman away in Jamaica, the oldest member of the church now was Brother Hawkshaw. A stocky amiable bull-necked man, Brother Hawkshaw wore a tight waistcoat and black suit, and possessed a wonderful praying voice, hoarse and soulful. When he collected the offering and prayed over it, the church would first sing and then hum a chorus, timing it so that the soft soothing hum would act as a background to the spoken prayer. He and his best friend, silver-haired Brother Plummer, took turns at collecting offerings. Brother Plummer was a more relaxed person than sternly upright Brother Hawkshaw, but he too could give an offering a poetic blessing.

One Sunday, Pastor Spring called Brother Hawkshaw up to the front of the church to be honoured. The Spring daughters lined up beside him in their role as 'Heaven Harmonies' and prepared to sing.

'We all love Brother Hawkshaw, don't it?' the Pastor asked, to sounds of general agreement. 'We must love and honour him now, for he is old, and may not be with us always.'

In soft haunting voices, the Spring girls sang a repetitive chant: 'Death has a time – to carry you away.'

I could see that Brother Hawkshaw didn't like this very much, although he smirked and tried to look flattered. Sure enough, he was taken ill shortly afterwards, and was nursed at home by his devoted wife. Six months later, Brother Hawkshaw reappeared at church looking doleful. He had shrunk to skin and bone and his once-tight clothes hung about him. In happy surprise, Sister Dorothy congratulated him on losing weight. A week later, Sister Hawkshaw 'phoned the Pastor to say that her husband was dead.

Dismay met this announcement on Sunday, and Pastor Spring added that Sister Hawkshaw would welcome all church members to the Wake, to be held at her house. A traditional Jamaican Wake is known as a 'Nine Night', the ninth and last night of sitting up preceding the funeral. Like the bacchanalian Irish wakes of old, Nine Nights are growing less frequent, particularly in England. Songs and stories, often of an unusually bawdy nature, are told along with all-night hymn-singing and rum-drinking. There is a topsy-turvy atmosphere, for all the normal laws of life are suspended, an echo of Hallowe'en. The good self of the deceased will be presumed to be with God or awaiting judgment, but the bad self, a mischievous ghost called a 'duppie', might be present in the house and must be coaxed into leaving. Seeming irregularities in a Nine Night are for the naughty duppie's benefit. I have never been to a Nine Night, a custom renounced by Church of God members, who do not officially recognize the existence of duppies. However, I was to find that a little Nine Night topsy-turviness had rubbed off on the Hawkshaw Wake, even though it was only a Seven Night affair.

Near the narrow terraced house where the Hawkshaw family lived, fruit-laden stalls had been set up outside Indian shops. Lights blazed, their cables strung along makeshift awnings, and delicious sweetmeats sizzled over brazier-bucket fires, barbecued chunks of meat and roasted sweetcorn. Happy, excited faces beamed towards me from brightly dressed crowds who were celebrating the end of Ramadan. In the Hawkshaw home, when I eventually found it, festivities of another kind were taking place. Young 'unsaved' members of the family had prepared a banquet downstairs, where chicken, reggae and rum bottles greeted all-comers. Cars continually pulled up outside, as well-wishers queued to ring the doorbell.

'Sister Hawkshaw is upstairs,' I was told.

I had an awful premonition that Brother Hawkshaw himself would be laid out for all to see, but I was wrong. Instead, his widow sat up in bed, speaking on the 'phone to her sister in Jamaica. She seemed shaken, but pleased to have company.

'Don't worry 'bout me, the Pastor is right here now – in this very room,' she assured her unseen relative.

She was right, for Pastor Spring and the church deacon were sitting on the end of the bed, roaring with laughter at a Lenny Henry film on television. The joke concerned a West Indian funeral, with the coffin falling all over the place. The Spring girls and other members of the church greeted me from various parts of the large eiderdown-covered bed on which they perched. Sister Hawkshaw looked up from her pillow and gave me a nod.

All of a sudden, a big man in a blue suit burst into the room as if in terror, and shouted out, 'The duppie come!'

Then he shook with laughter and said, 'Only me lickle joke, you know. I come straight from a night club, 'cos me not a yard man, me never go home! Hello, everybody! So the old man gone, eh? Too sorry, but it happen all the time. I just come to pay respects. Me children bring the message, or me stay out till 4 am. Pastor, excuse me lager can, I think it spill.'

He was welcomed to the gathering, and sat heavily on the bed, leaning over to prim Arlene Spring, who remained polite with seeming difficulty.

'I don't believe in all this God and Heaven business, do you?' he asked, then launched into a comic story in strong 'patois', using the word 'oonu', which means 'you-all'. Nobody seemed very offended by this behaviour. A yard man is a stay-at-home, since 'yard' in Jamaicanese means 'house and grounds'. I decided to leave for my own yard, and bade the company farewell. As I left, the company began to sing with pathos: 'Farther Along, We'll Know All About It.'

At the end of the week, I was summoned to the funeral by a grey card, and so presented myself at church amid black-clad mourners. Everybody present had gone over to the English custom of wearing black for a funeral. In the Caribbean, however, white is frequently worn. My neighbour Sister Ruth had worn white for a family funeral, the veil hanging over her eyes, only a year or two ago. Young people have almost scoffed this custom out of existence.

When I reached the Church of God, I found that the service had already started. Two anxious young undertakers, black-clad with shoulder-length blond hair, at once turned to me and asked for help.

'Look, they made us put the coffin down at the front of the church, with the lid off,' one of them told me. 'We're s'posed to wait for the Pastor's nod, then go in and close it up. When's 'e likely to nod, d'you reckon? There's a programme on this card, but all the events are happening in the wrong order! Look, the choir is supposed to be singing, but they 'aven't even *got* here yet.'

'I think everyone here has to pay respects to the body,' I said doubtfully. 'The Pastor won't nod till then.'

So saying, I took my seat and mimed the words everyone was singing, 'When I've Gone the Last Mile of the Way'. Brother Hawkshaw had certainly walked his last mile. In his life, I had always been glad to meet him, but now I had to summon up all my courage for the long walk down the aisle to the open coffin.

Arlene Spring, immaculately dressed and coiffeured, stood stiffly on the rostrum and solemnly read out a 'Eulogy' on Brother Hawkshaw. She had written this herself, with a great deal of agonizing, and it sounded very impressive. Brother Hawkshaw had been born in 1911, he had worked for a sugar company in rural Jamaica, then emigrated to England in middle age. Details of his marriage, children, his work in transport and his loyalty to the Church followed. Sister Hawkshaw listened with bowed head. Prayers followed, then a sermon by a Bishop of the Church of God. Like all such bishops, he wore ordinary clothes and was addressed informally as 'Brother'. He knew Brother Hawkshaw well, and made a sincere eulogy of his own.

Arriving in haste and slight disarray, the choir took their places and the band struck up a monotonous rhythm. Everyone rose and left their seats to walk around the large church and say goodbye to Brother Hawkshaw. Sister Hawkshaw, her children, her grandchildren and other relatives stood beside the coffin, all crying softly. The rest of the church filed past slowly.

Brother Hawkshaw had been smartly dressed for the occasion, but his body looked limp and empty. Plainly the real Brother Hawkshaw was not at home. Only in his face did a trace of spirit remain. More than a trace, in fact. His eyes were open, and he looked both shocked and angry at this thing that had happened to him. He had faced death with incredulity.

Before I reached my seat once more, I noticed a grizzled old man with white-flecked eyebrows and moustache, mournfully playing a harmonica. The Pastor gave his nod, and the coffin was sealed.

'We will sing the Closing Hymn from the memorial card, and then make our way to the Burying Ground,' announced the Bishop. Guitars and drums rang on a sharper note as the song began.

> To Canaan's land I'm on my way.
> Where the Soul of Man Never Dies!
> My darkest night will turn to day
> Where the Soul of Man Never Dies!
> No sad . . . farewells.
> No tear . . . dimmed eyes.
> Where all . . . is love.
> And the Soul of Man Never Dies!

This old 'country hymn', well-loved in the southern states of the USA, was once a favourite in Elvis Presley's circle. The gaps in the lines (which I have copied from the song card) accurately show the rhythm. As I left the church, I noticed a battered guitar propped in a corner.

At the 'Burying Ground', I soon found the Church of God party of mourners gathered around an open grave. Two young gravediggers, also West Indian, stood stripped to the waist, spades at the ready. A mountain of flowery wreaths, mostly white, lay nearby. Brother Hawkshaw was gently lowered down on canvas straps, and clods of earth and a few wreaths dropped upon him. Then the young men worked with ferocious energy, filling up the grave once more.

'You know there's unemployment, when young men have to take a job like this,' someone remarked. 'Once it was only old people who would work as gravediggers.'

'Me knew it would come to this – me see black washing hanging from line,' an old lady mourner observed.

When the grave was levelled, the flowers were heaped on top, all the mourners lending a hand. Hymns were sung from a songbook at first. To my surprise, the old, white-eyebrowed man I had seen earlier then took over the singing, which became traditional in character. He had fitted his harmonica on to a frame joined to the battered guitar, and danced from foot to foot as he played and sang in a style reminiscent of a mournful Jimmy Reed. Among the sombre, black-suited mourners, he wore an open-necked lumbershirt, and seemed a being from another age. This is the song he sang:

> No Grave Can Hold My Body Down!
> No Grave Can Hold My Body Down!
> When the trumpet shall sound
> And the dead in Christ shall rise.
> No grave! (No grave!) No grave!
> No Grave Can Hold My Body Down!

As the plaintive harmonies poured forth, Brother Plummer leaned forward, plunged his right hand into the mass of flowers, and made the motion of shaking an old friend's hand in parting.

'Goodbye, Brother Hawkshaw!' he exclaimed twice, very clearly.

Who wrote that haunting song, 'No Grave'? I have heard it sung by hillbillies in the Smoky Mountains of Tennessee. My mother, on an epic trip across the Kalahari Desert in 1990, heard the same song hoarsely whispered in English by her Tswana guide, George Lekaukau, as he fetched sticks for the fire that kept lions at bay. Jackals yelped and howled in the nearby darkness as if joining in the singing.

The Funeral

I don't know when my death will come.
I don't know when my death will come.
It may come in the night.
It may come in the day.
I don't know when my death will come!

CHAPTER SIX

Traditional Music in Church

I like the old time preaching,
Praying, singing, shouting;
I like the old time reading of God's word.
I like to hear those old time 'Hallelujah! Glory!'
I like the old time worship of the Lord.

Joining in the Chorus

Where do choruses, repetitive mini-spirituals, come from? They seem to be in the very air a West Indian Christian breathes. One chorus, which seemed to blow into the Church of God on a holy breeze about five years ago, begins, 'It's me again, Lord! I've got a prayer that needs an answer!'

Ten years ago this chorus first sprang into being as a prayer that *received* an answer on a lonely road in South Carolina, USA. The prayer was uttered in those words by the Reverend F.C. Barnes (Pastor and founder of Red Budd Holy Church, Rocky Mount, North Carolina) when his car broke down and he sought rescue. Before help came, the prayer had become a song, and the Pastor later recorded it for an obscure gospel record company, 'Consolating Sound'. Firstly the song conquered America's 'Black Churches', then it came to England, more through word of mouth than by record. Reverend Barnes, a silver-haired, good-humoured man, looks rather like a Jamaican to judge by his photograph. He and his church sing traditional spirituals, and the Red Budd choir has a large following.

When a London primary school staged a 'Caribbean Night', a Church of God gospel group, complete with drummer, were invited to entertain the parents and children. When I arrived, the Church people were sitting around looking embarrassed as the school children danced to 'sinful' Trinidadian soca records. Barbadian Church of God members are less puritanical than Jamaicans over secular music, as a rule. The church Music Director was a tall, forceful young lady of Barbadian descent. Nevertheless, she looked relieved when the soca ended and the gospel music began.

I could see that the children, (whose parents came from Africa, Greece, China, Ireland, India and England, as well as from the Caribbean) enjoyed seeing real live musicians and singers. As the chorus began, they started to dance again. My friend the Music Director ran to the microphone, and noisily showed them how to stamp on Satan:

> Lower, lower – stamp Satan lower! Lower, lower,
> Lower, lower, lower, lower!
> Higher, higher – raise Jesus higher . . . .

Finally, one of the most popular choruses in the Church of God was sung, to great acclaim.

> I'm bound, I'm bound
> For Higher Ground!
> I'm seeking a golden crown!
> Can't remain – on ordinary plain,
> I'm bound for Higher Ground!

This song, repeated over and over again, nearly brought the school down. While it was still going on, the Music Director joined me at the soft drink stall. I asked her about the origins of Church songs.

'That's a West Indian song,' she said. 'Some of the choruses are American, but the rhythms are all West Indian. Only choir songs are sung exactly like in America.'

Sometimes a phrase in a Church of God sermon reminds someone of a chorus. First one Sister begins to hum, providing a background to the speaker. Others join in. Still the Pastor preaches on. Then the hum turns into words, which rise until the preacher realizes his voice is not alone, and he stops in mid-message and starts to sing along. Last of all, the church men and boys join in, and the message has become a chorus.

Once Pastor Spring was speaking about the end of the world. 'I'm telling you! Better get your business straight! We shall not be here always! Time is winding up!'

There and then he seemed to preach a chorus into existence, one that I had never heard before.

> Better get – your business straight!
> Time is winding up!

On another occasion, the Deacon was speaking in moving tones of Christ's agony, carrying the Cross slowly uphill. As he spoke, an eerie wailing hum arose from the Sisters, and soon everybody was swaying and singing mournfully.

> Lonely road! Lonely road!
> Calvary's way is a lonely road.

The choruses in Bishop Noel's Mount Zion church have a haunting, traditional Trinidadian and Grenadan character. Invariably, they lead to holy dancing and speaking in tongues.

'These choruses and spiritual songs are a great comfort to us,' the Bishop once declared.

A verse from the Bible is often quoted in all the churches I describe:

Let the word of Christ dwell in you richly in all wisdom: teaching and admonishing one another in psalms and hymns and spiritual songs, singing with grace in your heart to the Lord. (Colossians 3:16)

St Paul's remarks to 'the Colossian brethren' have served a second purpose – providing a name for a type of song, the Spiritual, or Negro Spiritual. In 'camp meeting days', in the American South, a hymnbook entitled *Spiritual Songs* was often used. 'Classic' spirituals, of course, evolved by word of mouth, since slaves were seldom allowed to learn to read or write. I have rarely heard the word 'spiritual' alone used in any of the churches I describe – usually it's 'spiritual songs'.

Both spirituals and choruses are sung in Mount Zion. Here are just a few of them. You must imagine these songs sung mostly by middle-aged women in turbans, with bongo drums or tambourines thumping a slow, steady rhythm. Strange wails, heartfelt groans and 'scat singing' harmonies provide a background to the words.

> Adam in the Garden hiding.
> Hiding, hiding!
> Adam in the Garden hiding.
> Hiding from the Lord his God!

> 'Adam, where art thou?'
> 'Adam, where art thou?'
> 'Adam, where art thou?'
> 'Hiding from the Lord my God!'

'Oo-ooh-oh!', a strange chant once arose, like the introduction to the spiritual 'Deep River'.

> Mother, oh mother, the train has almost gone!
> Mother, oh mother, the train has almost gone!
> Mother, oh mother, the train has almost gone!
> So buy a ticket and sail away to another shore.

Perhaps the train had been a ship in an earlier version. Tambourines stepped up to double rhythm, but the slow, stately voices remained at the same soulful pace.

'Go Down Moses' is sung in its entirety at Mount Zion, with Caribbean verses I have never heard anywhere else. (Although I use the word 'spiritual' to mean a traditional Christian song from American Southern plantations, church members have no knowledge or interest in the origins of the songs, but sing them because they like them.)

Solo: I believe without a doubt.

Chorus: Let my people go!

Solo: A Christian has the right to shout!

Chorus: Let my people go!

Very few West Indians who sing these songs realise that the long-ago American composers hid between the lines a message of earthly hope for freedom from slavery. Some English-born young people refer to slavery times at the Church of God, but to many middle-aged and elderly West Indian churchgoers such talk smacks of sedition and blasphemy. I have heard a preacher at a Church of God Revival hold the congregation spellbound for two nights, only to lose them all on the third night by mentioning 'racism' and preaching on the theme, 'Go Down Moses . . . Let My People Go'.

Go the people did, and the preacher stood aghast at the end, amid empty seats. Although slavery is a semi-taboo subject when raised consciously, the subject seems to raise itself unconsciously whenever old spiritual songs are sung at a crowded Revival, to the music of electric guitar, drums and saxophone. Tears begin to pour down, a misty Holy Ghost feeling descends, and whole congregations shake in a weeping swaying perfectly timed dance.

Sister Angie, the Church Reporter, once wrote: '''Standing In the Need of Prayer'' was sung, and a Spirit of Travail descended.'

I well remember that occasion, as the singing was so loud that I found myself able to join in without upsetting the rhythm.

It's me! (It's me!) It's me, oh Lord!

Standing in the Need of Prayer!

Not my Pastor, not my Deacon, but me, oh Lord!

Standing in the Need of Prayer!

Another old spiritual, sung both in Mount Zion and the Church of God, carries a note of scarcely bearable sadness, the rolling sorrows of a people and the Spirit of Travail. Shivers run up and down my spine when I hear it.

> Where shall I be when the First Trumpet Sounds?
> Where shall I be when it sounds so loud?
> It sounds so loud it can wake the very dead!
> Oh, where shall I be when it sounds?

Still in Mount Zion, we shall leave Bishop Noel with a song that sounds very like a blues. In fact, there is a blues of the same name (recorded by Guitar Slim).

> The Things I Used To Do, I don't do those things no more!
> The Things I Used To Do, I don't do those things no more!
> I have seen many changes since the day that I was born!
> I have seen many changes since the day that I was born!
> The roads I used to walk, I don't walk those roads no more!
> The roads I used to walk, I don't walk those roads no more!
> The roads I used to walk, I don't walk those roads no more!
> The Things I Used To Do, I don't do those things no mo-ore!

Celestial Songs

In the Yoruba Celestial Church of Christ, choruses are seldom sung. 'He is King of Kings. He is Lord of Lords!' is fairly popular, a song known in the Church of God and among white English evangelicals. There are few tambourines in the Celestial Church. A musician told me that long ago the Yoruba speaking-drums had bells attached. Were these the first tambourines? Moors from North Africa brought tambourines to Europe.

(The finest tambourine I have ever seen stands in the museum at Perth, in Scotland. It is twice the size of a modern tambourine, with a wooden bar across the middle, hung with bells. In the eighteenth century, it was played by an African soldier who led all the processions of the Band of the Perth Militia, performing wild acrobatics and never missing a beat.)

The blue *Spiritual Songbook* used in the Celestial Church bears scant resemblance to its American predecessor. For example, many of the words of songs are in both English and Yoruba. Comparing the two languages, I was interested to see the word 'God' translated as 'Olorun'. 'Olorun' is the traditional name for the Yoruba Supreme Deity, or Creator, showing that to Celestials the old ways blend easily into the new faith of Christianity.

Yoruba hymns, however, translate oddly into English, with titles such as 'The World Is Bent All To One Side', and 'God is in Charge of the Vehicle'. A favourite song, sung to quavering flutes, organ and trumpet, has a tune similar to the student ditty 'She Was Poor But She Was Honest'.

> Witches are all confounded.
> The wizards are all confused.
> Satan trembles, even crumbles.
> Before Jesus' mighty power!

On a Wednesday night, a stern Warrior Shepherd warned us about music.

The devil was in charge of music in Heaven, and when he fell, he and the rebel angels took music down to earth with them. Lucifer was jealous when he saw Adam given the task of naming all the animals. So he thought he would destroy men with music . . . .

But on Friday Father Peter, the church leader, announced that the church orchestra would play secular jazzy rhythms at the Church Dance next day, held at a nearby hall.

'Do not wear soutanes or church clothes, but come dressed for dancing! My only rule is "No see-through clothes". Saturday we boogie!'

Traditional Instruments

One moonlit night, I was walking through Tottenham's Broadwater Farm Estate, where my sister used to live. I encountered a giggling group of young Ibo ladies from Nigeria, dressed in white robes. They were 'witnessing' (evangelizing) to residents of the tower-block estate. Most notorious council estates are visited regularly by African or Caribbean church teams, God's unknown social workers.

'We belong to the Worldwide Holy Sabbath of Christ the King Mission,' I was told eagerly. 'Do come along next Saturday! That is our Sabbath Day.'

On Saturday, my sister I and were welcomed by tall, easy-going young Joe Tabansi at the door of a Church of England vestry used by the Ibo church. Although African churches each tend to become associated with a particular tribe, it would be unthinkable for anyone to be turned away for tribal reasons. Nation-states, not tribes, could be termed the Curse of Africa, since they are an alien form imposed upon an unwary continent.

We kicked off our shoes in the tiny entrance hall and peeped into a room full of white-robed worshippers. Joe, the helpful President of the Church Youth Association, was also dressed in a long white cotton gown. While a beturbaned Pastoress addressed her flock in musical Ibo, Joe whispered a few words of instruction.

'Do not wear black. It is the colour of the spirits of evil,' he said, a rule that applies in a great many West African churches. 'We believe that the seventh day of the week is Saturday, and that each day begins at sunset. We fix sunset at 4 pm, since that is the time the sun sets in, er, some parts of the world. They are just praying now, so let us go inside.'

We tiptoed in and found ourselves in a cosy village-hall type room furnished with long movable benches. White-clad members prostrated themselves in prayer, and we heard the gentle bump of foreheads on floor.

Smiles of welcome greeted us when prayers were over. In amazement, I gazed around at the many musical instruments that lay around, ready for use. All were hand-carved out of hard, white wood, in rough-hewn chisel-marked fashion. I recognized slit-gongs, the speaking drums of the Ibo people.

'We call them Ekay,' Joe whispered.

Traditional Ibo slit-gongs can be beautiful objects, carved to resemble animals, stained and polished in a black and tan hue. These ones were functional pieces of wood. Nevertheless it was astonishing to see London-made slit-gongs at all. Each gong resembled a long shallow bowl with a handle at either end. Instead of being hollowed out, like a real bowl, two deep square cuts had been incised from the flat, wooden, tray-like surface, connected to one another by a narrow slit. Knobbly twigs did duty as drumsticks. Another sort of slit-gong, resembling a small wooden coracle boat, was also in use. Small drums of peeling goatskin rested beside red shaking-calabashes covered in beads. V-shaped cowbells completed the orchestra. Impatiently, I waited for the music to begin. Joe gave us a list of church events, and I read, 'Church HQ, Nnobi, Nigeria. High Priest: Most Rev. M.N. Amakaeze.' My eyes roved around the rapt worshippers. Some of the white robes were of silk, with faint spotted patterns.

> Man made God! Man made God!
> I never can believe that Man made God!

As soon as this oddly-phrased but ultimately reassuring song began, musicians picked up instruments and the tiny room filled with joyous, lighthearted music. Long tall Joe played first on goatskin drums and then upon two twig-like sticks, clacking them fervently together. Booming notes rolled from the Ekays, wonderful instruments which responded to the tap of a slender curved twig as if alive. Half the Worldwide Sabbatarians played, the other half danced, with ecstatic cries of 'Holee!'

Chant-and-answer, or call-and-response, gospel songs in Ibo increased the sense of oncoming miracles. My sister found it hard to stay still in her seat.

Finally, to my regret, the bendy African 'jack-knifing' dancing ceased, so did the swaying and the music. The capable Pastoress gave the announcements.

'At Pentecost, I want you each to bring two loaves, one candle and one candlestick, as well as fruit for sacrifice. We shall now have prayer and testimony.'

One by one, members came forward, sang a short Ibo hymn, then told their troubles to the church. Most of the troubles concerned immigration problems, passports and visas. Examinations also proved a terrible 'oppressor'. The Pastoress not only prayed over the people, but promised to give practical advice afterwards. This Ibo Pastoress was rather brisk. After each testimony and prayer, the testifier performed a solo song and dance to the music of Joe's drums.

'Stop singing in Ibo – you are doing it incorrectly!' commanded the Pastoress, eyeing an English-born girl sternly. 'What you are singing doesn't make sense. Sing it again in English.'

Looking flustered and foolish, the poor girl gave a nervous giggle and complied. A stout woman who prayed for a safe journey to Nigeria brought four large bowls of fruit as an offering (or 'sacrifice') to God, and laid them on the altar. After many chanted prayers, the musicians took up their sticks and hollowed chunks of log, and drumming began anew.

Five collections were made (interspersed with holy dancing), a churchgoer's nightmare. Last of all, after tithes, came the angel's fee. Everyone danced around the overspilling collection plate, and then holy water was sprinkled over the money as a blessing. Some of the prayers were spoken in 'pidgin', a language as incomprehensible to me as Ibo.

'Angels are here!' cried Joe Tabansi, as an unexpected and beautiful organ solo rang out to accompany the last hymn. Afterwards, the men put the wooden instruments away, women cooed delightedly over one another's babies, and children ate up most of the fruit dedicated to a safe journey to Nigeria.

'Come again!' smiled Joe.

Gospel Music

Revivals, in the Church of God, resemble amateur gospel concerts, relays of singers and musicians interspersed with preachers. Amateur gospel music, where passion and feeling replace slickness, is often superior to the professional variety. 'Revival gospel' is performed by mixed groups of all ages, the middle-aged to the fore. Songs from Jamaica alternate with Country and Western ditties about 'the boll weevil in my cotton, Lord'. Sometimes an American song is sung in a West Indian accent, or a Jamaican chorus is introduced by American-inspired music. Revivals are held in large churches, and are advertised by word-of-mouth in a hundred Pastors' Announcements. Church members of all ages attend, together with 'unsaved friends' who may 'find Jesus' at the Altar Call, when swaying masses sing softly, 'Oh, Holy Ghost – Revival comes from Thee.'

Sometimes a particular song takes a revival by storm, as happened on the day when a group of stout and radiant women took the stage and sang to the accompaniment of impassioned young men with drums and guitars:

> I'm a soldier – let me ride!
> I'm a soldier – let me ride!
> Lower down, chariot, let me ride,
> I'm riding on the billows for home!
> I'm working on the building,
> It's a sure foundation,
> I'm holding up the bloodstained
> Banner for my Lord!

Gospel Music

I'll never get tired
Of working on the building,
'Cos I'm going up to Hea-eaven
To get my reward!
Now, if I was a smoker, I'll tell you what I'd do!
(*A Voice:* Tell me!)
I'd give up smoking and go to working on the building too!
And if I was a preacher, I'll tell you what I'd do!
I'd keep right on preaching and working on the building too!

At this point, applause drowned out the words, so the singers danced as the band played on. Older church members may have been reminded of the time in the early 1960s when they rebuilt the roofless church, Sunday by Sunday, singing as they laboured. When 'Working on the Building' was over, the congregation stayed on their feet, clapping to the invitation 'Come on in this house'. Only the very old, or those with babies or sleeping children, remained seated among the coats flung over pews and chairs.

Standing at the station, come on in this house!
Standing at the station, come on in this house!
Standing at the station, come on in this house –
Come on in this house and praise the Lord!

The Celestial Church of Christ

The Celestial Church of Christ, founded by S.B.J. Oshoffa (1909–85) is a West African church. Members wear white robes known as 'soutanes'. Mainly attended by Yoruba people from western Nigeria, this church has flourishing offshoots in Paris and New York, as well as in West Africa and Britain.

A Harvest Festival is proclaimed open in the Celestial Church of Christ, Elephant and Castle, London (*opposite*). 'The Elephant' is full of Nigerian churches of every kind. At this 'Harvest', announcements are made not only in English and in Yoruba, but also in French for the benefit of a visiting Celestial Church from Paris.

A dance of Thanksgiving (*above*). Guests wearing traditional robes watch the happiness and fervour of the dancing.

While the band plays (*left*), Senior and Superior Evangelists, men of high rank in 'Celestial', rejoice and dance. 'Celestial music', with its unique blend of thick-toned gospel trumpet, ethereal church organ and thudding Yoruba drums, will surely one day be recognized as a triumph of 'black music' on a par with early jazz.

'Harvests' reflect the importance of crops to West African villagers (*above right*). Among the extravagant decorations, a lone candle burns 'by Divine command' in the centre of the doorway, a custom peculiar to Elephant and Castle. A staff across the doorway bars newcomers until prayers are over and the kneelers arise.

Worshippers bring their tithe-offerings of candles, money or perfume to the altar. The Sister in the foreground (*right*) said it had been revealed to her that she should pray with a candle and water, and then offer them to God in thanksgiving.

The Naming Ceremony for the new-born is an age-old Yoruba tradition, but the fruit is a Celestial innovation (*above*). Seven types of fruit celebrate the baby girl on the eighth day of her life. Clad in white, she is held by a Prophetess, who while in a 'spirit trance' gives her both a name and a life-prophecy while her father tape-records the proceedings.

A remembrance service for the Founder, Prophet Oshoffa, symbolized by an empty coffin, is held at a new 'Parish' in London's East End (*opposite*). Oshoffa's son, Evangelist Ebenezer, kneels in prayer as a scribe records the prophecy of the man 'in spirit' behind him.

Women pray to the left of the centre aisle and men to the right. Sugar and honey are offered to the worshippers to symbolize the sweetness of life.

In the hope of a message from God, a member lies in a trance (*above*) on the sand of Mercyland, which represents the sacred West African beach of Porto Novo.

Overleaf: **Worshippers at 'Cele' must leave their shoes** outside the church (Exodus: 3, 5). As Mrs Ojara, wife of Chief Ojara, leaves the Seventh Year Parish in London's East End, her chauffeur deferentially returns her shoes.

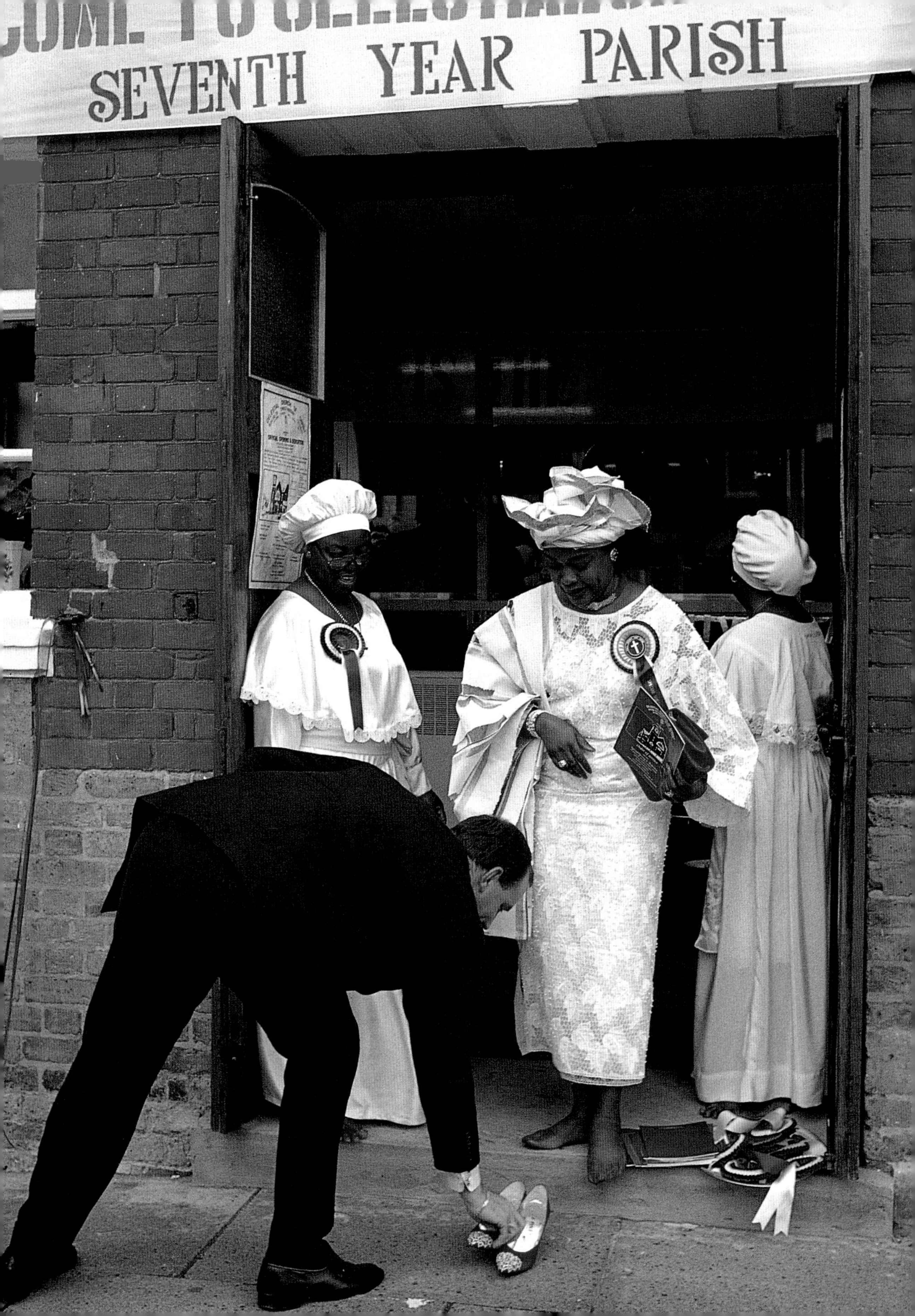
SEVENTH YEAR PARISH

CHAPTER SEVEN

That Christian Jubilee

No more strangers as we walk this land;
No more strangers, for Christ has made us one.
Sharing with others – the message of the Cross.
For we are no more strangers in God.

(CONVENTION THEME SONG, BRIGHTON, 1991)

The National Convention in Brighton

Every July, proprietors of hotels and boarding houses in Brighton smirk with satisfaction as they contemplate rows of ticks on their Advance Booking charts. Every room filled! Once more, it is Church of God National Convention Time! Members of Britain's two largest Church of God 'families', the New Testament Church of God and the Church of God of Prophecy, usually hold four-day Conventions within weeks of one another. Coaches transport the faithful from every major city in England and Wales to the Brighton Centre, a vast auditorium hired at great expense. Each Church of God invites speakers from its counterpart ('Prophecy' or 'New Testament'), and some Convention-goers attend both occasions. Here are some leaves from my Convention Diary.

WEDNESDAY NIGHT

Suddenly the Adastral Hotel, where I am staying, is transformed into a buzzing, lively night-spot, filled with laughter and loud Caribbean voices. Young Brothers and Sisters from Bristol, Cardiff and Bradford make the most of their yearly treat. I can hear late-night excursions to the pier being planned, with many a knock on many a door. Everyone is dressed to the nines, even the elder brethren who turn in early.

THURSDAY MORNING

Today, most of the breakfast tables are occupied by still-cheerful, unhung-over young people in bare feet and dressing gowns, chattering happily in Birmingham accents ('I never saw your posse last night, you know'). Later I get over to the Centre, where the National Overseer (a kind of Archbishop) declares the Convention open.

To the Centre, where the Mayor of Brighton, with obvious delight, welcomes the Conventioneers and describes the many attractions the resort has to offer.

Most of this Convention seems to consist of reports, appointments, finance statements and other committee business. Funds have been raised for Missions in Africa, particularly in Sierra Leone. Thus a tradition that began in 1800 is continued, for some of Sierra Leone's earliest missionaries were ex-slaves from Jamaica. Food and clothing, as well as Bibles, are sent abroad. Sheltered housing and hostels have been opened for needy church members in England. Disaster funds have been raised for the victims of earthquakes, floods and hurricanes in the Caribbean. British charities have also received contributions. Most of the money for such efforts comes from entry fees to church gospel concerts.

A thirty-year-old mother gives a graphic account of her suffering from sickle cell anaemia. She is lucky to be alive. Every few months, all her blood has to be replaced.

'Imagine a razor being dragged through all your veins,' she tells the audience, who shudder with pity and horror. I am not sure that money for medical research is always usefully employed, but at any rate a lot of it has been raised today. Only people of African descent suffer from this terrifying and usually fatal condition.

'I had to stay in the maternity ward for weeks, and then leave on crutches,' she says. 'How I envied the other mothers, who walked out holding their babies!'

A happier note is struck by the reports, given with cheerful formality, of the many Church Camps held in the countryside. Children file on stage and each takes a turn at the microphone.

'We were camped right out in the bush,' a little girl from Bradford says with awe, using her parents' term for a Caribbean forest.

'When we were in Devon, the local people had never seen coloured people before,' a teenage girl remarks, with rueful humour. 'They asked if they could pose for photos with us, and ruffled our hair, but I could see that they meant no harm.'

SATURDAY

It appears that we Convention-goers are not expected to stay in our seats all the time. We consult the programme and attend those occasions that interest us. The rest of the time, we can sit talking and sipping soft drinks in the halls of the plush Brighton Centre, or chatter our way up and down the seafront, in and out of souvenir shops. 'Church of God Rock' is on prominent display, in sticks of all colours and sizes. Some Convention-goers have saved all year in order to occupy suites in the very grandest of Brighton hotels. When two acquaintances meet, one from Sheffield, the other from Wolverhampton, they run towards one another with loud cries of 'Brother So-and-So!', hug, kiss necks and shake hands fervently. A moment later, after an exchange of platitudes ('So when you reach?'), they calmly part for another year.

In the lunch hour, enormous queues form at Foray's Cafe in Boyces Street, the favourite Convention eating-place. No wonder, for the roasts and puddings are out of this world! Thirty years ago, I used to frequent this cafe with a calypso-singer friend, huddling round the coal fire in winter. Little did we think that one day nearly all the customers would be West Indians (in Convention season) and the two rooms of Foray's would ring with loud Jamaican conversation. ('Coffee, please, and make it white. Appearances are deceptive!')

Chris Eubank, the Jamaican-born boxer, lives in Brighton. Accompanied by his Christian mother, he takes the Convention stage after lunch, and pretends to fight one of the Pastors. The Pastor pointedly displays 'the other cheek' until his neck aches. Needless to say, this show meets with wild applause. ('Hit him, man!')

The Church of God missionary to Uganda, a white Englishman married to a Jamaican, suggests, from the Convention stage, that church members should visit patients in psychiatric hospitals. This excellent idea is well-received by the Convention, although I doubt if the hospital staff will be equally as enthusiastic. Such patients are encouraged to 'go out into the Community' when their hospitals close, but the Community (or public) have seldom been invited inside to meet *them*.

'We must be more out-going!' the missionary persists. 'Our church has not healed itself yet. The reality of life in England was such a shock that people who came here felt wounded, and sought spiritual healing in church. But that was thirty years ago! We must heal ourselves, before we can heal others.' (Doubtful applause.)

It occurs to me that, in England at any rate, the Church of God is a Protective Church. In my definition, a Protective Church is one that sees the world outside as threatening, and the Church as a place of safety, where members nestle happily beneath the sheltering Wing of God. The other sort of church is a National Church, where 'We' are the majority. The 'Protective Church' mentality can be found in its extreme form in the Islam of Bradford, where the sinful world of white people is feared to the point of hysteria. In Pakistan, the same Islam becomes a unifying, almost worldly, National Church.

England has its National Church, the Church of England, yet the true 'official belief' of the white English is Economics. Ever since the television-induced 'satire craze' of the early 1960s, cynicism, cruel humour and sneering have become second nature to many English people. As the unpleasing smell of stink bombs, thrown by hooligans into a Convention doorway, assails my nostrils, I understand why the Church of God has become a Sanctuary from 'the world'.

Unlike the missionary to Uganda, Bishop Arnold can well remember the early days of the church in England. From the balcony, I can see hundreds of Sisters' hats bobbing in approval as he addresses the Convention. As most of the wide-brimmed hats are white with black crowns, they look like enormous cartoon eyes staring up at me.

'We thought we came to England to make money!' Bishop Arnold cries, with great emotion.

'Didn't make any, though,' a young Sister, in the seat behind me, remarks. Obviously she has been affected by English cynicism.

'But God had other plans!' the Bishop continues. 'When we saw the *moral apathy* so many of our people had sunk into, we, my friends and I, felt God had called on us to act. Who can remember those days when we walked in the rain from bedsit to bedsit, preaching, getting together in rooms with one paraffin stove, pleading with backsliders – remember? No fitted carpet then, no car outside! Cold lino, shared sink and toilet on a dark landing! We say, ''Look where God has brought us,'' but have we lost our spirituality? Anyway, that is how we began. We had no education, we knew nothing of ''counselling''. Who needs ''counselling''? We need *prayer!*' (Enormous cheers, and no wonder. The jargon of 'counselling' has begun to invade even such a haven of King James' Bible English as the Church of God.)

To shouts of 'Truth! Truth!', Bishop Arnold describes the church's progress. Unlike those West Indian preachers who copy Black American sermons on slavery and civil rights, and empty whole churches in the process, Bishop Arnold touches skilfully on racial matters. Discreetly, he hints that Christians need not be shy or timid towards white people, nor snobbish towards West Indians from different islands.

'Too many of us suffer from Islandism! Some even suffer from Parishism: "What parish in Jamaica you from?"'

Amid clapping and laughter, the Bishop next condemns all 'colour snobbery'.

'The colour is the house the soul live in, but the soul has no colour!'

Outside the auditorium, passers-by must be wondering if that is clapping they can hear, or the whole roof of the Centre falling in.

SUNDAY

Early in the morning, the gaily dressed members of the Women's Missionary Band march with banners and music up and down the Brighton seafront. On this last day of the Convention, we all crowd in to hear the National Overseer's address. A white American with a flamboyant wife, the Overseer is treated by church members as royalty. His presence is a reminder of the church's early days in the hillbilly log cabins of the North Carolina mountains.

'Now don't all crowd at once – form a queue or I shan't sell you souvenir pictures of myself no more,' his wife addresses us tartly.

After the Overseer's Message, everyone waits with bated breath as the list of pastors is read out. Every year, a few changes are made. Pastors are normally well-loved and few members welcome re-organization. Changes are received with gasps of surprise, but accepted as the will of God.

With a rap of his gavel, the Overseer closes the Convention, and everyone streams from the building. Luggage is heaped up, and coaches set off homeward. Young people in the back of my coach, still in the grip of Convention fever, rattle tambourines. Soon everybody is singing that year's Convention Theme Song.

> Sign me up for that Christian Jubilee!
> Write my name on the ro-oll!

I've been changed since the Lord has lifted me:
I want to be – ready when Jesus comes!

In 1992, the Church of God Convention was held at the Birmingham Indoor Arena for a change. When I arrived, a speaker was reading the story of Ezekiel raising the dry bones. He announced:

I was a Dry Bone before I met the Lord! Yes, the unsaved are like dry bone, or dry coconut, with no vitality of inspiration in them. Remember dry coconut back home, you elder brethren? You have to grate it to get the oil out. A job I hate, as I cut me hands! Yet those Dry Bone raise up and join when Ezekiel cry. When we spread the word, we raise up the dry bone! We must do it right! The hip bone don't join to the head bone, or the ankle bone to the neck bone, or that would be Deformity!

(*A Voice:* My, Ezekiel done a lot of preaching!).

On cue, a middle-aged Sister in mauve, with a white hat, took the microphone as the band tuned up.

> Ezekiel say!
> Can these Dry Bones live?
> Prophesy, prophesy, and hear the word of the Lord!
> Toe bone to the foot bone,
> Join together!
> Foot bone to the ankle bone,
> Join together!
> Prophesy, prophesy, and hear the word of the Lord!

Lesser branches of the Church of God family hold their conventions in large churches hired for the occasion. District (as opposed to National) Conventions, emotional and highly musical occasions, also take place all over Britain. These resemble well-attended Revivals.

Bishop Noel's Mount Zion Spiritual Baptist Church enjoys a week-long Convention every summer, held out of doors at a busy corner of the Harrow Road. Other churches of the 'Mount' family come down from the North, or out of the West, and the Convention usually consists of fifty or sixty conventioneers.

Mount Zion's Convention is at its most delightful at dusk, at the close of a fine summer's evening, when the smell of stale beer drifts from the open door of the 'Frankfurt' pub and idlers from that hostelry drift dreamily to the wide bit of pavement where the altar table stands. There, my tall friend Barbadian Mitch among them, they drape themselves across the metal kerbside railings and nod their heads to the tambourine rhythm in profound wooziness. Mount Zion candles burn brighter as the sky slowly darkens. Eventually an electric torch and a flickering Dickensian lantern join them among the flowers and holy water bottles on the table.

Holding an election-style megaphone, Bishop Noel barks Bible texts at the mildly curious crowd, and issues commands to the assembled Marys and Josephs, as he now terms the brightly robed Brothers and Sisters. Young Meshach, a tall twelve-year-old boy in a smart suit, stands wide-eyed, thumping a tambourine. His face shines with devotion to duty, with occasional flashes of humorous subversion. A stout Mary in a gown of vivid blue beats rhythmically with a white wand on a small flat drum, her eyes staring, entranced. Harmonizing hums behind the preaching show that a song is forthcoming.

> John saw them coming! John saw them coming!
> John saw them coming – all dressed in white!
> They all were numbered! They all were numbered!
> They all were numbered – all dressed in white!

Meanwhile, white youths on skateboards glide carelessly by, and pedestrians stop a while and smile. Non-gliders receive tracts, and thank the earnest Mothers and Marys politely. A trio of fashion-conscious boys jaunt by, all of Meshach's age, yet sporting extraordinary hairstyles – flower-pot-shaped brushes rising abruptly from shaven scalps. Proudly, they glance at their reflections in shop windows, and I feel like singing 'I'm a Pink Toothbrush'. Instead, I wave goodbye to the Bishop and walk away as a new, yet strangely familiar, song about John emerges from the humming. It is a song I remember from my skiffle days.

> John said the city was just four square!
> Walking in Jerusalem just like John.
> And he declared he'd meet me there!
> Walking in Jerusalem just like John!
> I want to be ready. . . .

Thanks to the research of Sam Charters in the American South, I know that the song that I once believed to be of hillbilly origin is actually a variant of one of the first Negro spirituals ever to be transcribed, 'Walking in Jerusalem Just Like Job'. Even the usual 'Bluegrass banjo' backing to the song, Charters reveals, is a style brought to Kentucky by West African slaves. Yes, I enjoy Mount Zion Conventions, and not just for the preaching.

The Celestial Harvest

The Celestial Church of Christ, as far as I know, does not hold Conventions, but refers to church get-togethers as Harvests. These Harvests occur at intervals between August and November, a time of year that coincides with the Nigerian yam harvest. Bunting hangs from the ceiling, more fruit than usual is heaped up for the offering, and cans of soft drinks are passed around. However, I cannot interpret the booming Yoruba songs and sermons, and can only describe the tip of a tropical iceberg.

Below the surface loom ancient Yoruba practices Christianized, notably the yam festivals of West African villages. A Celestial Harvest is a joyous occasion where musicians get together and everyone dances and exchanges gifts. Let Homer Sykes's photographs speak for themselves.

CHAPTER EIGHT

Testimonies and the Holy Spirit

I am determined
To hold out to the end!
Jesus is with me,
On Him I can depend!
And I know I have salvation,
For I feel it in my soul.
I am determined to hold out to the end!

Testimony Time

Testimony Times are a feature not only of the Church of God, but of virtually all West Indian and black American churches. Oprah Winfrey, the Mississippi-born television personality, I am sure, learned the art of managing a discussion programme in a little country church at Testimony Time.

There are few regional differences in the Church of God in Britain, despite the miles that separate Leeds from Manchester, Bristol from London. The Midlands are famous for their choirs and musicians, however, and the churches in Wales have a unique 'matiness'. White people frequently attend services, and the playful jokiness of young South Welsh workmen, epitomized by the singer-comedian Max Boyce, has spilled over into the church. In a tiny, dark little chapel in a narrow side-street near Bute Town, Cardiff, nor far from the docks, I listened to Brother Erroll's testimony. Brother Erroll's Cardiff accent contrasted strangely with that of his gentle old Jamaican father, who looked on admiringly.

Jesus is the sweetest name I know! Who is like Jesus? He's my rock, my sword, my shield – He's my wheel in the middle of a wheel! Without Jesus, I could never have made it to where I am! You know, I really enjoyed my time at school, like, but I was so looking forward to leaving and getting a job. I prayed – boy, I prayed!

When I was sixteen, and I learnt I'd got a job in electrical engineering, I was so happy I went dancing down the road! The works Treasurer was a good man, and he encouraged me. But everyone said that the boss hated black people, and I realized, like, to my grief, that it was true. He put me to work alongside four white youths who made my life a misery! I just turned to Jesus and prayer.

Month after month, I prayed, and things began to happen. One by one those youths left, replaced by kind-hearted people. Last of all, the boss himself left, and my friend the Treasurer became boss! So we should all thank Jesus!

Judging by Testimonies, the avowed aim of most Church of God members is to 'make it in' (get to Heaven eventually) and to bring along as many converts as possible. There is an unstated feeling that being good is not merely a means to an end, but an end in itself. One summer's evening, I overheard two stout middle-aged Jamaicans in overalls talking as they burrowed into the motor of a broken car. One, who was a churchgoer, addressed the other.

'All you wants to do, to become a Christian, is to have repentance. You must truly repent o' your sins, and then you got to give up tiefing, cussing and fighting.'

The other looked dubious, as if he wasn't sure whether or not the sacrifice were worth it. Worldly middle-aged Jamaicans are usually genial old boys whose lives outside work revolve around the pub, betting shop and domino table. Their English-born sons are subjected to worse temptations, and many Church of God members feel that they have a special Mission to Black British Young Men. The opportunity of playing music in church seems to be the bait for many young men.

Outside my Nigerian friend Esther Abiona's Redeemed Church of God, a noisy crowd of Cockney children were playing around the doorway.

'Are you going in?' they asked me, incredulously.

'Yes, are you coming?'

Six of them followed me, the oldest a girl of ten. Politely, they refused the offer of a front pew from the usher, and sat in a row on a bench at the back, speaking in whispers. At Testimony Time, a young man declared, with some truth, that 'the whiteman has forsaken his belief in God'.

This may have been true of the children, as after the service, I noticed that they were absent. For myself, I was puzzled that one Church of God (like this one) could be all-Yoruba, another (like Pastor Spring's) almost all Jamaican and Barbadian. Yet the style of service was the same. Could the average Church of God in England be termed a Jamaican National Church? Within the Moslem faith, a faith that prides itself on its uniformity, one London mosque caters for Arabs, another for Turks and a third for Bengalis. It would be possible for a Moslem to enter 'the wrong mosque' and so feel ill-at-ease.

Instead of saying 'Church of God', I tried saying, in my mind, 'the Yoruba Church' and 'The Jamaican Church'. 'Yoruba Church' sounded almost right, although the Celestial Church and many others of wildly different type also cater for Yorubas.

'Jamaican Church' definitely sounded wrong, especially as Pastor Spring occasionally sent members from door to door, pleading with Indians, Ethiopians, Chinese and English people to attend a Revival. Once, when he managed to persuade several such Eastern people to attend, he preached such an atypical hellfire sermon, born of last-throw desperation to convert the heathen, that he frightened them all out again. In a sense, many a Church of God is Jamaican by default, as much as by inclination.

Testimony Time at Bishop Noel's church, Mount Zion, is particularly interesting whenever the Bishop himself testifies.

This he did one day, but as Testimony Time was announced, he noticed a woman kneeling at his feet in a trance of prayer. Taking a truncheon painted in black and white zebra patterns from one of the brethren, he gently used it to stroke the woman. Then he raised her to her feet and kissed her on each cheek, turning her head with his own burly forehead.

'This is a Holy Kiss,' he announced to the church. 'Last night I fasted and went down into the valley, the valley of bones. There I met Ezekiel, and he showed me the Holy Kiss.'

A latecomer came in at that moment, a woman in crimson robes. She walked over to the centre pole, where candles flickered on the beribboned sunwheel, and kneeled briefly to the holy tree. Then she took her seat, as Bishop Noel began his Testimony.

Greetings to the Household of Faith! For my Testimony, I would like to recall the day I went into a trance. I felt ill. Mother Ivy was with me, and I found later she went and fetch a doctor. But at the time I didn't know nothing 'bout that.

An Angel took me, and we flew over green hills, over many places and dangers. At last we came to a tunnel! 'Do not fear,' the Angel whisper, for I think I pass through Hell.

There in the dark, scientists and homosexuals approached me, but I held the Angel hand real tight and said, 'Get away from me with your vile attentions!'

I saw the tormented and pitied them, and at last we came to a green meadow with a mansion. The Angel told me it was the Place of Rest. I signed my name in the book, and I felt so glad and so peaceful to be there. You know, I wanted to stay for ever, but they said 'You must go back for now, but you will return later.' That was nineteen years ago, and I'm still waiting.

When I awoke, the brethren was all around me, and the doctor said my breathing had been slow. I had been in a trance.

Several Sisters, who had been summoned to the Bishop's bedside on that long-ago day, loudly assented, nodding and saying, 'That's right! I remember!'

I looked from turbaned Mother Ivy to the many pots of trailing ivy in the church. Bishop Noel ended his Testimony, declaring that although 'Jehovah Wickedness' (Witnesses) say that only one thousand and forty four souls can go to Heaven, he had seen many more in the Place of Rest, a Place where he longed to be.

My reverie was broken by a sprightly, elderly Sister who walked up to the Testimony spot, singing loudly.

> Oh John, oh John, what do you say?
> Walking in Jerusalem just like John!
> That you'll be there at break of day.
> Walking in Jerusalem just like John!

Taking her stance, she gave a Testimony consisting entirely of song titles and spoken fragments of songs, just as an announcer at a 'soul' concert builds up a performer by stringing together phrases taken from his greatest hits.

Brethren, we walk that Lonesome Valley, we got to walk it for ourself, but at the end of the valley, we find Peace in the Valley! Up above my head, I hear Music in the Air! Angel are right on spot! John Saw Them Coming! They all were Numbered, all dressed in white!

As the church led off into one of my favourite songs, 'Peace in the Valley', I closed my eyes.

The Holy Spirit

All the churches I describe in this book have one thing in common – belief in the Comforter, or Holy Spirit.

To be possessed, or 'filled', by the Holy Spirit is the final proof of God's grace. In Bishop Noel's Mount Zion and in the Celestial Church of Christ possession comes easily, at every service. Not only the Comforter Himself but angel powers of other kinds may descend. But in the Church of God, as in all Pentecostal Churches, for all the races of mankind, the Comforter, Holy Ghost or Holy Spirit descends *occasionally*, conferring a great blessing, even on those who do not fully feel His Power. Some attend church for a lifetime and are never 'filled', only 'sanctified', the first sign of the Holy Spirit's presence in a person.

Pentecostal Churches are, of course, named after the Day of Pentecost, when the Comforter first made His appearance. In Chapter 14 of St John's Gospel, Jesus prepares the disciples for His departure, but makes them a promise: 'And I will pray the Father, and he shall give you another Comforter, that he may abide with you forever.' (St John, 14:16); 'But the Comforter, which is the Holy Ghost, whom the Father will send in my name, he shall teach you all things, and bring all things to your remembrance, whatsoever I have said unto you.' (St John, 14:26).

Nowadays, the first sign of sanctification is often identified as a convulsive jerking of the backbone. Complete Holy Ghost possession manifests itself by 'tongues' and holy dancing, leaping, running or shaking on the spot. Such is 'extreme possession' – for others the Comforter arrives and Comforts quietly.

As He spreads His way from person to person, until the church is in an uproar, the Comforter is greeted with joy. Sometimes He appears at the climax of an emotional Message, forcing the preacher to run from the pulpit and leap into the air. At other times, He appears when a driving, searing song coaxes His presence, first noticed when screams ring out among the congregation.

Let me take you to the Church of God and introduce you to the Comforter.

One night, not long ago, Brother Clarendon was playing the drums, young, fervent Florence Spring played the keyboard, and the rest of us sang a song from the hymn book.

> In shady green pastures, so rich and so sweet –
> God leads His dear children along.
> Where the water's cool flow bathes the weary one's feet –

God leads His dear children along.
Some through the waters, some through the flood!
Some through the fire, but all through the blood!
Some through great sorrow, but God gives a song –
In the night season and all the day long. . . .

At this moment, there was a scream, and elderly Sister Hamilton cried 'Oh Glory! Glory!' The words of the song grew ever more faint, as singer after singer succumbed to the Spirit, and shouted aloud in tongues, ran on the spot, shook, juddered stiffly or wheeled around with angel-wing-arms outspread. Eerily changing her tune, Sister Florence played the same notes over and over again, a repetitive rhythm that led one after another of the calmer Brethren to welcome the Comforter with His own greeting-song, slow and plaintive:

Welcome, welcome, welcome the Holy Ghost.
Holy Ghost, we welcome you.

'Come with power!' somebody added, and so He did.

'It was like a rushing wind!' Pastor Spring breathlessly remarked afterwards. For twenty minutes, Holy Ghost pandemonium reigned, a misty, tragedy-laden phenomenon, where through a fog I could vaguely see Sister Spring stalking the building, fervent-eyed, tapping on a tambourine and chanting:

Come, Holy Ghost, come!
Come, Holy Ghost, come!
Write my new name
With your quill on my heart!

Finally the Comforter left for His home Above and things slowly returned to normal. Prayers thanking the Holy Spirit arose, and Pastor Spring announced, 'We have been greatly blessed.'

Who is the Comforter? Is He the Holy Ghost, or an outbreak of mass hysteria, or both? Scholars often point to the similarity of Holy Ghost possession with the 'possession by spirits of the ancestors' that is a feature of most African religions. Those of African descent certainly find it easy to experience Holy Ghost possession. Are invisible ancestors present when the Holy Ghost descends? My friend Evangelist Steadman, once a pupil of Bishop Noel, claims that when she speaks in tongues, West Africans can understand her. She implies that she is speaking in the forgotten language of her forefathers. It would be interesting to learn whether or not the oft-repeated Comforter phrase 'Shula Mamai' occurs in a West African language. Although I feel the presence of Another when tongues are spoken, one could just as well say that when Africans think they are possessed by their ancestors, they are *really* being possessed by the Holy Spirit.

Holy Ghost possession was noted by Wesley, and has occurred in England long before the arrival of West Indian and African immigrants. Charles Dickens mentions an English 'jump up' church in *Dombey and Son*.

... The admonitions of the Reverend Melchisedech had produced so powerful an effect that, in their rapturous performance of a sacred jig, which closed the service, the whole flock broke through into the kitchen below and disabled a mangle belonging to one of the fold.

All religious belief assumes the existence of a spiritual realm invisible to most mortals. Does the Comforter come from within or does He enter from outside? The same question could be asked of Good and Evil. Do good and evil only live within the human heart, there to grow or shrink, or do they live, personified as God and Satan, in mysterious realms such as Heaven and Hell? I believe in the latter theory. When a surge of kindness and love overwhelms the soul, does this not come from God? Where does an evil thought come from? The Holy Ghost manifests itself in a way that, to an observer, is neither good nor evil, although the dancers and tongue-talkers afterwards speak of feeling blessed and honoured. Nevertheless, the Holy Spirit too may dwell outside humankind between visitations.

Such problems appear never to perplex Pastor Spring, for every month he fills in a printed form, to send to his bishop (or 'overseer'): 'New members. Saved, 4. Sanctified, 3. Filled with Holy Spirit, 2.' Then he signs it and posts it on its way.

Mount Zion Spiritual Baptist Church

There are only a few Spiritual Baptist churches in Britain, most of them heavily influenced by the ebullient personality of Bishop Noel from Grenada. Many members are Grenadan, but West Indians from every part of the Caribbean, including Jamaica, attend Mount Zion. The style of worship is similar to that of the Zion Churches of southern Africa.

On the morning of Mount Zion's annual sea-baptism service, a blindfolded candidate (*opposite*) is led towards the waiting coach that will take the church from London to the beach at Felixstowe. Bishop Noel, Founder of the church, is on the left.

Safely arrived at Felixstowe, Bishop Noel leads his elders to the beach (*above*), where they prepare to set up an altar. Scattering holy water, he sanctifies the seashore.

Still blindfolded, the baptismal candidates (*opposite, above*) are plunged three times beneath the waves, in the names of the Father, the Son and the Holy Ghost. Blindfolds are then removed.

The end of a perfect day. Bishop Noel relaxes (*opposite*).

Within his candle-lit church, Bishop Noel (*top*), flanked by Mother Twila (Mrs Noel) on his left and Mother Joyce, addresses his flock.

MONTHLY
FROM
A WARM
FREELY WE
IN JES

for there is
NO
DIFFERENCE
for all have
sinned and

Mother Twila rings the holy bell to drive out the evil spirits before prayer (*above*).

Mother Twila (*previous page*), her staff with spirit-writing hanging from her wrist, anoints a penitent with Holy Oil; he falls to the floor in a trance and is exorcized by Bishop Noel. In the background is the centre pole and the prayer wheel with candles alight. To try to awaken the Brother from his trance, a cross is laid on him (*opposite, above*). The church grows anxious. Suddenly, purged of all evil influences, the redeemed penitent raises his arms and sings to the glory of the Lord. A relieved Mother punches the air with joy.

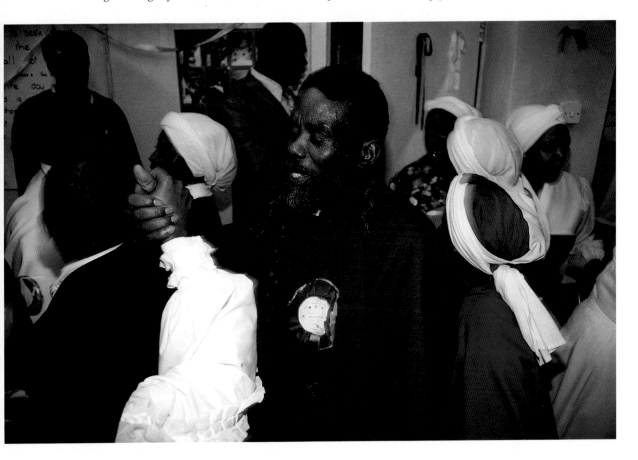

Evening worship over, Bishop Noel warmly shakes hands with all the members of the congregation (*above*). Everyone greets one another with murmurs of 'God bless you'.

Overleaf: **Farewell, Bishop Noel!** Founder and mainstay of the church, the Bishop died just as this book was nearing completion. Mourners pay their respects around the open coffin, to the sad sweet strains of 'Swing Low, Sweet Chariot'. Mother Twila lifts each child-member across the body in turn, as a gesture of love and respect. Later, a steel band will lead the church in procession to the burying-ground.

CHAPTER NINE

I Shall Wear a Crown

When the Battle is Over, I shall Wear a Crown!
I shall Wear a Crown! I shall Wear a Crown!
When the Battle is O-ver, I shall Wear a Crown
In the New Jerusalem!

(CHURCH OF GOD CHORUS)

The Church Play

This is a chapter of Unusual Events, and one such event is the Church Play, when members can dress up in gleaming angel wings or wear silver-paper crowns in anticipation of the New Jerusalem. Only young people take part in plays, which take place at Revivals and Youth Conventions. Most such plays have only one act, and are known as Skits or Sketches. My favourite actress is young Florence Spring, the Pastor's daughter, who can do a 'wicked' imitation of an old Jamaican lady talking in 'patois'. Old and young, in the audience (or congregation) fall about with laughter whenever she opens her mouth. Nevertheless, such plays are meant to point a moral, often a very simple one (as in the play where a girl 'backslides' from church and automatically goes to prison, apparently for no other reason).

Sometimes miniature Biblical epics are staged, complete with crucified Jesuses and Weeping Marys. To my mind, the audience seems faintly embarrassed by these, as if feeling that such portraiture may be blasphemous. On one dreadful occasion, at a Revival, a youth tried his hand at being a gospel comedian. In parody of the well-known preachers' command to 'turn to your neighbour and shake his or her hand', he loudly announced: 'Now turn to your neighbour and spit in his eye!'

This was not well received. Until that moment, no one had realised that the young man was *meant* to be a comedian. Even the young man himself had second thoughts on the matter, for he broke into a sweat, muttered something about being 'back later' and disappeared forever.

'Me sorry for him, you know,' an old lady remarked.

At Moss Side, Manchester, on the night when I crossed the road from the Brotherhood of the Cross and Star to the Church of God, I saw a most enjoyable play in the latter church. The church was a large one, its spire visible from afar. Spiked railings around it testified to the sad prevalence of crime and vandalism in the district. A recent television documentary had made heavy weather of Moss Side drug peddling and gangsterism.

Fittingly enough, the Youth Play showed Satan as a gang leader in dark glasses calling a meeting of his henchmen, a miscellaneous collection of Moss Side 'rude boys'. Lights went out, and in the huge wood-panelled Mock Tudor church only the stage was spotlit. A large wall-mirror at the back of the rostrum reflected both the players and the appreciative audience, adding an extra dimension to the scene. The young people played to a full house, one that hung on their every word.

First of all, the rough young henchmen roistered around like street-corner youths as they waited for the boss to arrive. Bang! A huge gangster-like character burst in and ordered the demons to explain their lack of success. Only then did we in the audience realise the Hellish nature of the scene. Called to account, the demons blustered, boasted and put the blame on one another, as they tried to excuse their incompetence at abolishing Christianity. Their accents were Moss Side Jamaican, and had the audience in stitches.

'When that Herod coom oop, I hardly needed to tempt 'im: 'e was bad as me! That Herod! Bwoo-o-oyy!'

'Yes, but the Enemy struck back with Martin Luther and Wesley! Only you, Demon Communism, have done a good job!'

Communism smirked and studied his fingernails, little knowing that his day would come.

Youth Conventions

Youth Conventions, like Revivals, are joyous occasions in the Church of God. Young people from a group of local churches sing, play and preach to congregations of all ages. Rehearsals take place for months before the event, and the largest church in the neighbourhood acts as the venue. A visitor might be surprised to find the whole church dancing. Such dancing is happy and carefree, not the poignant, tragic judderings of Holy Ghost possession. I have been waltzed out of my seat by jolly old ladies on such occasions, where smiles and holy kisses abound.

Brother Clarendon is in much demand on the drums, and if Brother Ray the saxophone player from Birmingham is present, all Heaven is let loose.

Last year, when I looked in at a Youth Convention, a group of four girls were singing, repeating the same three lines over and over again, as guitars rang and the notes of a tenor saxophone pierced the air.

> Jesus is a-coming! And He won't be lo-ong,
> Time to get started
> On the way back home.

Young people linked arms and swayed, shouting, 'All *right!*' whenever the song began anew. A white couple who had wandered in stayed entranced for a while, but finally shook their heads, smiled ruefully and left. A month later, at a Revival, another three-line gospel ditty caused a sensation. Not a soul could sit down, and only the most conservative brethren were content to dance in their pews, shaking on the spot.

> I went to a meeting one night.
> And my heart wasn't right.
> But something got a hold of me.

But the biggest 'chorus sensation' I have ever seen was brought about by Sister Palmer, a forceful middle-aged woman who conducts open-air meetings at Harlesden's Stonebridge Estate. Almost casually, Sister Palmer announced to her fellow members of Tubbs Road Church of God of Prophecy that she had brought a new 'chorus' back from her trip to Jamaica. With a hollow Latin coconut-shell effect on drums, she began to sing, to a tune reminiscent of 'Merrily We Roll Along':

Such a fun to see!

Satan lo-ose!

Satan is a Loser Man.

A Loser Man, a Loser Man.

Satan is a Loser Man.

A Loser Man all the time!

Jesus is a Winner Man. . . .

And so on, for over an hour, until the deacon locked the church up for the night and people went dancing down the road singing aloud about losermen and winnermen, to the surprise of passers-by. Young Sister Angie from Barbados, who was not present, later said that she didn't know what all the fuss was about. 'We've been singing that song in our children's Sunday School for years,' she remarked.

Easter and Feetwashing

'Back home in Jamaica, at Easter time, we do all household work on the Thursday before,' Evangelist Steadman told me, as we sat in her little flat and sipped tea and evap. 'On Good Friday itself, we fast before morning-church, then come back for our home-made bun-and-cheese. Excuse me, Brother Roy, me head is haching.'

So saying, she adjusted her turban, took a knife and cut a potato-like slice from the Jamaican prickly-pear cactus that loomed over us in its pot. Slowly, she placed the slice on her brow (having first removed the

157

prickles) and assumed an expression of bliss. My grandmother had shown me this cure for headaches, using a slice of cucumber instead of a cactus.

When Good Friday came around at the Church of God, members jokingly asked one another, 'Have you brought my bun-and-cheese?'

Nobody was interested in hot cross buns. Instead, after the service, bun-and-cheese was served by Sister Dorothy. In Jamaica, as in West Indian bakeries in Britain, a 'bun' is a hard bun loaf. My slice tasted like raisin bread – delicious!

Not long after Easter, both the Church of God and the Mount Zion family of churches hold a 'Lord's Supper and Feetwashing', or Holy Communion. At the Church of God, Pastor Spring was taking the service, a very serious occasion. Voices were hushed, and an electric feeling of mystery, tragedy and anticipation could be felt. The altar table had been laid with an impeccable cloth. Pastor Spring is a tidy man, and in his Easter sermon he had read aloud, with delight, the Bible passage that describes Christ's linen as being neatly folded in the empty tomb. Crumbly white bread and dark red, alcohol-free wine reposed on the table in silver vessels, covered by a lace napkin, just as in a Baptist church. Chairs surrounded the table, and the whole church 'partook of the Supper' in three sittings.

One chair, at the head of the table, stood apparently empty. No one sat in it – no one visible, that is, for this was Christ's chair. Jesus Himself was the invisible host at His Own Supper.

'This do in remembrance of me,' Pastor Spring read in thrilling, emotional tones. 'Eat ye all of it!'

All ate the bread, purely in remembrance, and stared with awe at the chair where Jesus sat.

Then came the wine, and no one dared to breathe, as the Pastor cried in a voice of passion: 'Drink ye all of it! Drink ye all of it!'

Filled with strangeness and a sense of the sorrows of the world, we quickly left our seats and allowed the next eight Brethren to partake.

Next came the Feetwashing, a far more relaxed occasion. I have attended Feetwashings in Birmingham where trumpets, saxophones and drums boomed and swirled, and the whole occasion became a barefoot dance. Here we had only tambourines, so matters were more muted. In the Middle Ages, the kings of England had washed the feet, each year, of a few chosen humble subjects. Later, this custom changed, the subjects being paid in Maundy Money by the Sovereign 'in lieu' of feetwashing. Nowadays, the Church of England has forgotten feetwashing, but the Church of God remembers it still.

Modesty forbids mixed feetwashing, so Pastor Spring took charge of the Brothers at one end of the hall, while Sister Spring organized the Sisters at the other. Chairs scraped, and towels, aprons and large basins of warm water were carried to and fro. There were no screens, but the men resolutely turned their backs on the women, and began to remove jackets and roll up sleeves. Jackets were hung over the back of chairs. I dwelled on the Bible passages the Pastor had earlier read aloud.

He riseth from supper, and laid aside his garments, and took a towel and girded himself.

After that he poureth water into a bason, and began to wash the disciples' feet, and to wipe them with the towel wherewith he was girded.

Then cometh he to Simon Peter: and Peter saith unto him, Lord, dost thou wash my feet?

Jesus answered and said unto him, What I do thou knowest not now: but thou shalt know hereafter.

Peter saith unto him, Thou shalt never wash my feet. Jesus answered him, If I wash thee not, thou hast no part with me.

Simon Peter saith unto him, Lord, not my feet only, but also my hands and my head.

(St John, 13: 4–9.)

My reverie was interrupted by Brother Plummer, who handed me a

---

Church of God apron-towel, or towel tied to apron strings. So we sat down and washed one another's feet and dried them with the towels wherewith we were girded. From somewhere over in the feetwashing Sisters' domain, a chant arose.

> We will drink! We will eat!
> We will wash one another's feet!

Pastor Spring and young Brother Clarendon washed each other's feet with expressions of great care and humility, rubbing with their fingers in absence of soap and flannel. Over in the Sister's half, the washing had ended and loud tambourine playing had begun. I took a peep, and saw the four Spring girls dancing vigorously in a circle without touching hands, totally absorbed in the rhythm and the song that went with it. They looked like African village girls in a travel film, but the occasion was tense now, and un-holidaylike. The girls danced and the rest of the women broke into a fast chorus.

> Peter said we had to wash one another's,
> Wash one another's feet!
> Oh yes – washoo wash!
> Oh yes – washoo wash!
> Wash one another's feet!

Twenty minutes later, when husbands and wives, Brothers and Sisters, were all re-united, the girls were still dancing.

Prophecy

Tuesday evening in the Yoruba church, 'Celestial', is reserved for Prophecy. Members who attend are asked, 'Have you come to hear the Voice of God?'

If the answer is 'yes', the seeker for truth must not try to explain what he or she has come to hear. The Prophet or Prophetess is supposed to know that already. Tuesday Night Prophecy is a Christian version of a traditional Yoruba custom, divining the future by consulting an Oracle. In Nigeria's Yorubaland, only special diviners, members of a cult called 'Ifa' are able to prophesy in this manner. The Celestial Church 'diviners' are Prophets and Prophetesses who (as in Ifa) undergo a rigorous training. Cola nuts, essential for the chess-like Ifa divining, are forbidden under the strict Celestial rules for members. (These rules also forbid skin-bleaching, a harmful trait of fashion-conscious Yoruba women, and the wearing of black or red clothing.) Celestial oracles are angelic spirits who speak, in Medium fashion, through the prophet-diviners.

Sometimes, during an ordinary Sunday service at 'Celestial', a prophet becomes aware of an important unsolicited message. A doom is seen hovering over a blissfully unaware dancing Brother or Sister. When this happens, protocol is thrown away, and a prophetess can cross into the men's side of the church, and vice versa.

Once, when I was there, a Prophet became suddenly inspired, his normally genial features contorted with rage, and he rushed to a young man and bumped into him. Realizing what was happening, the young man fell to his knees in a pleading position, as the older person stamped with rage, shouted and shook his fists. Moses the Church Scribe rushed over and began to jot down the words of Prophecy as fast as they emerged. Message over, the Prophet slipped away and became once more an anonymous and well-behaved member of the congregation.

Neatly, Moses wrote out the Prophecy in Yoruba and English, and read it aloud to the victim.

'When you leave here, you will be run over by a car and so injured that *one arm* only will be able to move.'

The young man looked startled, turned cheese-colour and said, 'But it's my first time here!'

'Do not worry,' said Moses, reading on. 'Buy a candle, burn it all night on its side, and in the morning the fate will be removed forever.'

Greatly relieved, the young man made a bee-line for the candle-box. If indeed he were not run over, he would surely join the church for life, grateful for his rescue.

In the hope of a more soothing sooth-saying session than this, I turned up at the 'Celestial' church on a Tuesday evening. Father Peter, the church leader, welcomed me warmly and assigned me to Prophetess Porritt. I knew this Prophetess slightly. A large imposing woman, of light skin, she was not a Nigerian, but had arrived in London from the West Indies as a child. Her daughter, merry-eyed Jade, also attended the Caribbean-dominated Church of God, under Pastor Spring. To my surprise, the young man who had been saved from a road accident was behind me in the queue for the Prophetess. We conversed nervously, as if at a dentist's. He was surprised to hear that snakes lived in England.

'Pay twelve pence each for a candle,' we were told.

Crouching uncomfortably on the carpet, our lit candles dropping wax on to their tin-plate holders, we waited our turn and listened to the other Prophecies taking place here and there beneath the columns of the vast church. Possessed diviners kneeled beside the candidates for Prophecy and uttered strange whoops and cackles, like hyenas and gibbons combined. These sounds ushered in the spirit powers, and saw them out again. Moses the Scribe hovered here and there, waiting for a Prophecy to emerge so he could record it on specially-printed Prophecy paper.

'You won't have to wait long! Here is Prophetess Porritt now,' Father Peter encouraged us, beckoning to the buxom seeress. She wore a blue cape over her white robes – a sign of her prophetic calling. The church robes have a colour hierarchy – ordinary members wear white. Elders (or Shepherds) have yellow capes, and the highest-ranking colour is blue for Prophets.

'Oh no! I've done seven prophecies tonight already!' Sister Porritt complained, in a Cockney accent. 'Uncle! Surely someone else can do these two! My power is used up – this is ridiculous! Oh well, all right then.'

Taking a burning candle wrapped in palm fronds, she kneeled by my side and concentrated deeply.

'Nn-nn-noop! Noop! Noop! Noop!' she shrilled, then fell into a trance and spoke in guttural tones.

'The person behind the Prophetess-tess-tess-tess! Not this man – the person behind the Prophetess-tess!'

As she herself was the Prophetess, the spirit was speaking, not herself. It may have had to jerk itself out of her reluctant lips, but at least it had the sense to see that my presence there was frivolous. The real seeker for knowledge was the young man, the person behind the Prophetess.

'No, no – the man beside you!' Moses anxiously corrected it.

I kneeled, almost curled up, with my blue and white tin plate and wobbling candle, as Prophetess Porritt absently traced patterns on my bald head with one finger. Impatiently, the spirit barked out a message in faulty gramophone needle-language, then dismissed me.

'You do not, do not, do not – need to worry, worry, worry. Your path will, path will, path will – be made clear, ear, ear, ear,'

Gratefully, I took a clear path to the back of the church, where a tall young Prophet slowly recovered his own wits. Soon he was able to speak quite normally, with only the occasional convulsive 'Noop!' breaking through.

'Next week – Noop! – your Prophecy will be written out in full,' he told me.

So I left, with Prophetess Porritt and the nervous young man deep in a lengthy session of Prophecy.

In due course, Moses handed me my Prophecy, hand-written on lined paper with a printed heading: 'Notes of Spiritual Revelation.' My name and that of the Prophetess were entered under the headings 'For' and 'By', followed by the date. The Prophecy covered four sheets of paper, each signed at the foot by Moses. Here are some extracts:

Listen to the Voice of God to my son: the Lord is saying to you that He is able to do all things. I am the Lord that solves all problems. The Lord is saying to you, whenever you undertake any venture, first ask Him. And be careful whenever you want to sign anything. The Lord is saying you are his son, and whenever you want anything, you know how to ask him. Never be worried unnecessarily. Many things have to be shown to you in dreams. Pray for recalled memories. Never doubt your dreams. They are true dreams from me, your Lord God. Ask for my divine protection in all your travelling. God's Angels are with you – you are not alone. Peace be unto you my son. (Written by Moses)

Who could fail to be pleased with such a prophecy? The caution against signing anything is excellent advice for a writer.

Putting away my Prophecy, I glanced around the church where figures lay stretched under sheets here and there, burning candles at their heads and feet. Africans and many West Indians are used to sleeping with their heads beneath the bedclothes, a custom that may owe something to fear of marauding insects in the tropics. These particular sheeted figures sought divine protection. In their own side of the church, two women lay near one another, heads outside their sheets, talking like girls in a dormitory.

Father Peter walked by, addressed peremptorily by a kneeling woman – 'Mister!'

He leaned over and spoke softly.

'Thank you sar!' she beamed.

Feast Days

Bishop Noel's Mount Zion Spiritual Baptist Church, the ultimate 'Mount' church, holds many picturesque ceremonies. Feast days are common, with a banquet table laid in the church, with cloth, gleaming silver, flowers in cut-glass vases and masses of curried goat. Twists of silver paper are fastened to long loops of string to form decorations inside and outside, around the door. Woman visitors from other Mounts arrive in long pink frilly 'colonial Spanish' dresses, carrying parasols and wearing hats with immense, bobbing, blue-dyed plumes.

Children's birthdays, celebrated in church, resemble such feasts in their magnificence. Little Hannahbelle, in her plaits and best ribbons, celebrated her fifth birthday at Mount Zion around a table laden with fruit and soft drinks. Her cake had three swans made of icing on top. Everyone sang 'Happy Birthday to You', and I went home with a piece of cake wrapped in paper.

Later in the year, her brother Meshach enjoyed an elaborate church birthday party. Now twelve years old, Meshach has long been an ornament to the church, a suave Jeeves-like boy always dressed in a black suit. Fervent when playing a tambourine, he normally regards church-doings with an amused and indulgent eye. The banqueting table was laid for him, songs were sung and a delicious mixture of milk and honey was served in Communion cups. Just as in the Celestial Church, a line of robed figures paraded the building, each holding a handful of fruit. Most of the fruit ended up in front of Meshach, who looked gratified in a grown-up way.

Candles flickered, holy water was dashed about, and Bishop Noel, dressed in a black robe, held aloft the golden Lota vase filled with carnations. His wife stood by his side, one hand clasping a Roman-looking staff topped by a shiny metal star and a gold cupped crescent moon.

'Don't forget, brethren − Monday night is Mourning,' Bishop Noel proclaimed.

'What's that?' I asked Meshach. 'What do you do?'

'*We* mess about!' he said, gesturing at the other children. 'For the rest, it's like a prayer meeting.'

Christmas and Watchnight

At Christmas, all the churches I describe here hold parties, where spicy food and fizzy drinks are consumed in enormous quantities. Although the Jamaican-dominated Church of God strictly bans alcohol, more than a little rum usually finds its way into the Christmas cake.

On New Year's Eve, nearly all West Indian churches still observe a bygone Church of England custom – Watchnight. Services begin at about nine at night, with much prayer thanking God for 'preserving life' during the Old Year, and many pleas for Him to do the same in the New. At midnight, the services reach a peak of fervour, culminating in cheers and clapping. Sometimes soft drinks and Jamaica Patties are served, and then everyone goes home. Since public transport is hazardous on New Year's Eve, harassed pastors can be seen pushing more than the legal amount of old ladies into their cars, for lifts home.

Last year, I peeped through the door at Mount Zion Watchnight and saw the whole church performing an ecstatic 'ring shout' around the centre pole. A Mother came out, waved a red flag at the demon-haunted world outside, and then went in again.

At that moment, I saw three big old ladies in white hats walking anxiously in a row, shoulders touching, faces staring around, with expressions of extreme caution.

'Yes, we are lost,' one of them told me. 'Is where the Church of God hold the Watchnight?'

I took them to the Church of God door, where I was told, 'Thank you, sir! I am one hundred years old, and my friend here is a blind woman. When church over, we'll go home by train.'

Back at Mount Zion, I found their Watchnight to be almost over. Many of the Sisters stood holding burning candles. The open door of the church spilled light and laughter into the night. A staggering, jeering party of white youths reeled up to the church, where one of them dropped a box and broke two bottles of vodka. At once, all the revellers began to blame one another, with loud roars. One of the church elders eyed them apprehensively.

'The devil is a busy man,' he whispered to me.

A New Year had arrived.

Robing and Ordination Ceremony

Every few years, Bishop Noel of Mount Zion holds a Robing and Ordination Ceremony, where hitherto humble Sisters become Holy Mother Shepherdesses. Once ordained, they become imposing figures of awe and authority.

I took my seat in the dark but gaudily decorated little church and listened to Bishop Noel's introductory speech.

My apologies for all delays, but Candidates must always hold a private Feet-washing in the Sanctuary before the Examination. Before Ordination must come Examination, to make sure the Candidates are fit for the position of Mother Shepherdess. We West Indians are always late, but we go *on* till late, so don't be in a hurry to leave! You see here the rods and staffs, as spoken of in the Twenty-Third Psalm – 'Thy rod and staff they comfort me.' Shepherds must have rod and staff, innit? They are Shepherds, and need the tool of their trade. Natural shepherds use crooks to hook sheep, but Mother Shepherdesses will hook wayward souls.

The church was very full, everyone leaning forward eagerly to see what was going on. The four Candidates sat in the front row of chairs, facing the screened-off dais known as the Sanctuary. A table had been placed close to the centre-tree with its beribboned prayer wheel, and on this table lay a tall pile of neatly folded robes in rainbow colours. As always, there was ample space for dancing around the tree. Somewhere, a bongo drum pattered into life, joined by tambourines as 'a chorus was raised'. This particular chorus had been first raised, if not brought up, in the cabins of Appalachian 'mountaineers'.

> My Lord walked – this Lonesome Valley.
> He had to walk it by Himself.
> No one else could walk it for Him.
> He had to walk it by Himself.

Mother Twila, the leading Shepherdess, and other Mothers joined Bishop Noel and swayed slowly and rhythmically, as verse followed verse, the lines neatly overlapping. 'Brother got to walk – this Lonesome Val-lee', and so through Sister, Mother, Father until finally '*You* got to walk – this Lonesome Valley, you've got to walk it by yourself.'

Of the four Candidates, one was a man, soon to be ordained a Shepherd, a trusted assistant to the Bishop. One of the three women was elderly, the other two young, and all three wore white robes edged in patterned lace. The man wore a plain white robe. Mother Twila looked like a Saxon princess in a Victorian pageant. She wore a wimple-like sheet of silk, bright yellow in colour, held in place by a golden crown on her head, a crown studded with jewelled stars. Reflecting mysterious candle-light, the gold and jewels gleamed like real metal, not cardboard, paint and paper. In one hand, Mother Twila held a burning night-light in a jar wrapped in leaves and flowers. Bishop Noel wore full regalia, his hat alone the envy of many a Russian Orthodox Archbishop, I have no doubt.

'Lonesome Valley' had ended, but people still swayed in remembrance. Bowls used for the Feetwashing, and a silver coffee pot used for pouring Communion wine, were placed ceremonially around the base of the tree, forming a circular pattern, a basin in the centre. Some of the bowls were of handcarved wood, others were scooped-out gourds.

Gesturing at the pile of robes, the staffs, shepherds' crooks and wooden bowls, Bishop Noel declared that all of these had been made according to instructions given to him by God in dreams, after periods of fasting.

'Daniel, Chapter 10, tells us of three-week mo'ning and fasting,' the Bishop declared. Many of the children in my class at primary school had wondered why God spoke aloud to men in Old Testament times, but not nowadays. Here was the answer. Then as now, He can speak in dreams. Dreams are real, in the parallel worlds of the Old Testament and modern Africa, and Jehovah often gave His children elaborate instructions on how things should be made.

'Through fasting and mo'ning, I have learned many things,' the Bishop continued. 'But one should always question the Spirit! I have been offered beads, necklaces and all kind of things by devils' angels. At the name of Jesus, they throw them away and run! Ha! Many times people have tried to put voodoo on me, but I know they can't succeed! It is true, Israel! When I see people hung with chains, necklaces and beads, calling themselves ''Bishop'', I laugh! I have been through all that!'

Mother Twila by his side, the Bishop took a typed-out examination paper and began to read questions to the Candidates. Most of the questions were not on Biblical or doctrinal topics. They were solemn oaths, such as 'Will you promise to abide by God's law in Mount Zion?'

'I will!', 'I will!' answered each candidate in turn, all swaying still to the inaudible strains of 'Lonesome Valley'. Sometimes Bishop Noel made a jokey 'ad lib', but the would-be Mothers were too nervous or hypnotized to laugh. Each was declared a Shepherdess, and the man a Shepherd.

When the Bishop had finished, he asked the same questions again. On receiving the same answers, he solemnly intoned, 'Hold your peace.' Just as mourning and moaning were one, so were 'peace' and 'piece', for each time he intoned it, Mother Twila gave the Candidate a piece of robe, wand or turban cloth to hold. Soon all four examinees were staggering under the weight of mounds of folded blue and white clothes. They looked a bit like overburdened umpires at a cricket match.

Finally, the ordained ones were allowed to place their piles of robes and equipment around the base of the sacred tree, or centre-pole.

'Mo'ning and fasting led me to a Vision of the Garden of Eden, and of the many colours of the flowers growing around the Tree of Life,' declared the Bishop, gesturing towards the colourful heaps of robes.

Then each Candidate took a piece of cloth and tied it into a turban, white for the Shepherdesses, black and white for the Shepherd. One by one, they were told their new names by Bishop Noel.

'She is Mother Pointer. Now she will point the way. . . .'

Finally, holy water was scattered around the church from a jug, paper cups and hollowed-out gourds. Bishop Noel read from the Bible the tale of Jonah contemplating Nineveh from the shade of a gourd tree that God had planted. The ceremony ended with another chorus, remarkable for its eerie harmonies and spontaneous cries of 'Hallelujah!' that perfectly fitted the rhythm. Seldom have such simple words been given such an ornamentation, sung over and over again, in an ecstasy of throaty, soulful part-singing.

> Underneath the gourd!
> Underneath the gourd!
> Underneath the gourd
> The devil can't do me no harm!

Epilogue

We'll soon be done
With Troubles and Trials
Yes, in that home
On the other side.
I'm gonna shake glad hands with the elders
And tell my kindred, 'Good Morning!'
Then I'm going to sit down beside my Jesus
Gonna sit down and rest a little while.

Have West African and West Indian Christians overcome the 'Troubles and Trials' of prejudice and harsh treatment in Britain?

Once more, I was at the Church of God Convention in Brighton, at a three-hour gospel concert known as the Jamboree. Choir after choir took the stage, to mounting excitement. As in America's 'black churches', a girl soloist would stand apart, singing into a microphone. Some way behind her, a choir, frantically conducted by another young woman, would respond with a 'wall of sound', sometimes answering the soloist, sometimes backing her.

'Everywhere I go – everywhere I be – Jesus is mine!' sang the Tooting Choir.

Inspired by the driving rhythm of the band, young Sister Gloria Brown skipped to the microphone, sang like a Holy Ghost-possessed Tina Turner, and danced back to her seat. Old and young in the audience left their places and danced. A saxophone wailed and the two guitarists sat beaming, perched in small chairs, their feet tapping, like blues singers. In fact, at one point, Sister Watson the Music Co-ordinator had to rebuke them for playing a reggae rhythm.

I was reminded of the Jamaican evangelist, Mrs Starman, quoted by Zenga Longmore in her *Spectator* column of Brixton tower-block living, 'New Life'.

'Reggae music sends shivers and fires of lust searing through the human frame! Many a young girl led astray through this kind of music. The rhythms overpower the mind! It send you wild, dancing – dancing on a road to destruction!' (7 July 1990).

Simply change that rhythm by a few beats into gospel music, and she could just as well have said: 'Gospel music invites shivers and fires of Holy Ghost Power to go searing through the human frame! Many a young girl led to church through this kind of music. The rhythms overpower the mind! It send you dancing – dancing on the road to Salvation!'

So potent are the forces, or Supernatural Forces, attached to different rhythms by those who live and worship through music. The evening ended with the Mass Choir and the band pouring out a Mass Rhythm, while hats fell off and thousands of voices sang, 'The Storm is Passing Over – Hallelu!'

Outside, rain ceased to lash the promenade, and a star appeared in the sky, far out to sea.

Index

Page references in italics refer to the captions

List of Addresses

These are the addresses of the British headquarters of some of the churches mentioned in this book. The church leaders wish to emphasize that their doors are open for people of all races and nationalities to enter and worship God.

Brotherhood of the Cross and Star
Mill Hill Bethel
High Street
Mill Hill
London NW7
Telephone: 081 959 6606

Calvary Church of God in Christ
Northumberland Park
Tottenham
London N17
Telephone: 081 801 9318

Celestial Church of Christ
8 Harton Street
Deptford
London SE8
Telephone: 081 692 8320

Church of God of Prophecy
6 Beacon Court
Birmingham Road
Great Barr
Birmingham
West Midlands
Telephone: 021 358 2231

Lily of the Valley Mission
   International House Fellowship
33 Hay Close
Stratford
London E15
Telephone: 081 519 0469

Mount Zion Spiritual Baptist Church
29 Hazel Road
Kensal Green
London NW10
Telephone: 081 960 6528

New Testament Church of God
Overstone Manor
Overstone
Northamptonshire
Telephone: 0604 410 565

Redeemed Christian Church of God
St Mark's Church
Myddelton Square
London EC1
Telephone: 081 983 3221

Worldwide Holy Sabbath of
   Christ the King Mission International
13 Croydon House
Gloucester Road
London N17
Telephone: 081 801 5905

THE MUSIC

Black British gospel music is recorded on disk and tape by Sonny Roberts, managing director of:

Spindle Records
78 Craven Park Road
Harlesden
London NW10
Telephone: 081 965 8292